CIMA

OPERATIONAL LEVEL

PAPER E1

ORGANISATIONAL MANAGEMENT

FOR EXAMS IN 2018

BPP
LEARNING MEDIA

Fourth edition 2017

ISBN 9781 5097 1573 2
e-ISBN 9781 5097 1585 5

British Library Cataloguing-in-Publication Data
A catalogue record for this book
is available from the British Library

Published by

BPP Learning Media Ltd
BPP House, Aldine Place,
142/144 Uxbridge Road
London W12 8AA

www.bpp.com/learningmedia

Printed in the United Kingdom

Contents

Question and Answer index

Using your BPP Exam Practice Kit

One of the key criteria for achieving exam success is question practice. There is generally a direct correlation between candidates who study all topics and practise exam questions and those who are successful in their real exams. This Kit gives you ample opportunity for such practice throughout your preparations for your OT exam.

All questions in your exam are compulsory and all the component learning outcomes will be examined so you must **study the whole syllabus**. Selective studying will limit the number of questions you can answer and hence reduce your chances of passing. It is better to go into the exam knowing a reasonable amount about most of the syllabus rather than concentrating on a few topics to the exclusion of the rest.

Practising as many exam-style questions as possible will be the key to passing this exam. You must do questions under **timed conditions**.

Breadth of question coverage

Questions will cover the whole of the syllabus so you must study all the topics in the syllabus.

The weightings in the table below indicate the approximate proportion of study time you should spend on each topic, and is related to the number of questions per syllabus area in the exam.

E1 Organisational Management Syllabus topics	Weighting
A Introduction to organisations	25%
B Managing the finance function	15%
C Managing technology and information	15%
D Operations management	15%
E Marketing	15%
F Managing human resources	15%

The Objective Test exam

The Objective Test exam is a computer based assessment, which is available on demand at assessment centres all year round.

Objective Test exams in each level can be taken in any order, but candidates must pass all the OT exams for a level before they can sit the Integrated Case Study Exam for that level.

Each exam lasts for 90 minutes and the pass mark is 70%.

Results are available shortly after the test has been completed, and the results will include feedback.

The exam will be made up of different types of questions, including:

Question Type	Explanation
Multiple choice	Standard multiple choice items provide four options. 1 option is correct and the other 3 are incorrect. Incorrect options will be plausible, so you should expect to have to use detailed, syllabus-specific knowledge to identify the correct answer rather than relying on common sense.
Multiple response	A multiple response item is the same as a multiple choice question, except more than one response is required. You will normally (but not always) be told how many options you need to select.
Drag and drop	Drag and drop questions require you to drag a 'token' onto a pre-defined area. These tokens can be images or text. This type of question is effective at testing the order of events, labelling a diagram or linking events to outcomes.
Gap fill	Gap fill (or 'fill in the blank') questions require you to type a short numerical response. You should carefully follow the instructions in the question in terms of how to type your answer – eg the correct number of decimal places.
Hot spot	These questions require you to identify an area or location on an image by clicking on it. This is commonly used to identify a specific point on a graph or diagram
Drop-down list	Drop-down lists follow the same principle as multiple choice questions, in that you need to select one option from a pre-defined list. This can be used in conjunction with a gap-fill question: for example, you may be asked to key a numerical answer into a gap-fill box and then select an explanation for the approach you've taken from a drop-down list.

Learning Objectives

The table below has been prepared by CIMA to help you understand the abilities that CIMA is seeking to assess.

Learning objective	Verbs used	Definition	Example question types
1 Knowledge			
What you are expected to know	• List	• Make a list of	MCQ
	• State	• Express, fully or clearly, the details of/facts of	MCQ
	• Define	• Give the exact meaning of	MCQ
2 Comprehension			
What you are expected to understand	• Describe	• Communicate the key features of	Multiple Response
	• Distinguish	• Highlight the differences between	Multiple Response
	• Explain	• Make clear or intelligible/state the meaning or purpose of	Drop down list
	• Identify	• Recognise, establish or select after consideration	Hotspot
	• Illustrate	• Use an example to describe or explain something	Drop down list
3 Application			
How you are expected to apply your knowledge	• Apply	• Put to practical use	Multiple response
	• Calculate/ compute	• Ascertain or reckon mathematically	Number entry
	• Demonstrate	• Prove the certainty or exhibit by practical means	Hotspot
	• Prepare	• Make or get ready for use	Drag and drop
	• Reconcile	• Make or prove consistent/ compatible	Drop down list
	• Solve	• Find an answer to	Number entry
	• Tabulate	• Arrange in a table	Drag and drop

BPP
LEARNING MEDIA

Learning objective	Verbs used	Definition	Example question types
4 Analysis			
How you are expected to analyse the detail of what you have learned	• Analyse	• Examine in detail the structure of	Multiple response
	• Categorise	• Place into a defined class or division	Drag and drop
	• Compare & contrast	• Show the similarities and/or differences between	Hotspot
	• Construct	• Build up or complete	Drag and drop
	• Discuss	• Examine in detail by argument	Multiple response
	• Interpret	• Translate into intelligible or familiar terms	Multiple response
	• Prioritise	• Place in order of priority or sequence for action	Drop down list
	• Produce	• Create or bring into existence	Drag and drop
5 Evaluation			
How you are expected to use your learning to evaluate, make decisions or recommendations	• Advise	• Counsel, inform or notify	Multiple response
	• Evaluate	• Appraise or assess the value of	Multiple response
	• Recommend	• Propose a course of action	Multiple response

In your CBA, questions will be set which test up to the cognitive level of the verb in the component learning outcome in each paper's syllabus, so this means they will test up to level 5 verbs where the learning outcome permits this.

CIMA will limit the number of lower level questions in the exam – so that students will not be able to achieve the pass mark solely based on correctly answering knowledge and comprehension questions. Higher level questions, requiring candidates to demonstrate application, analysis and evaluation skills must be answered correctly for the pass mark to be reached.

Passing the E1 Objective Test exam

Tackling OTQs

- Read, and **re-read the question** to ensure you fully understand what is being asked.

- When starting to read a question, especially one with a lengthy scenario, **read the requirement first**. You will then find yourself considering the requirement as you read the data in the scenario, helping you to focus on exactly what you have to do.

- **Do not spend too much time on one question** – remember you should spend 1½ minutes, on average, per question.

- If you cannot decide between two answers – look carefully and decide whether for one of the options you are making an unnecessary assumption – **do not be afraid of trusting your gut instinct**.

- **Do not keep changing your mind** – research has shown that the 1st answer that appeals to you is often the correct one.

- Remember that marks are awarded for correct answers, and marks will not be deducted for incorrect answers. Therefore **answer every single question**, even ones you are unsure of.

- Always submit an answer for a given question even if you do not know the answer – **never leave any answers blank**.

- **Pace yourself** – you will need to work through the exam at the right speed. Too fast and your accuracy may suffer, too slow and you may run out of time. Use this Kit to practice your time keeping and approach to answering each question.

- If you are unsure about anything, remember to **ask the test administrator** before the test begins. Once the clock begins ticking, interruptions will not be allowed.

- Remember to **keep moving on!** You may be presented with a question which you simply cannot answer due to difficulty or if the wording is too vague. If you have only approximately 90 seconds per question, and you find yourself spending five minutes determining the answer for a question then your time management skills are poor and you are wasting valuable time.

- If you finish the exam with time to spare, use the rest of the time to **review your answers** and to make sure that you answered every OTQ.

Demonstrating your understanding of E1

The E1 examiner will expect you to demonstrate the following:

Broad understanding of business	It is important to ensure that you have a **good breadth** of **knowledge**, rather than having highly detailed knowledge of only a few areas.
Application of ethics, corporate social responsibility and sustainability	CIMA has identified these as important areas of study. They may be tested in a number of business areas, such as in organisational **culture**, **marketing** and **operations** as well as their application to **CIMA members**.
Awareness of contemporary issues	It is important to keep up-to-date with **current issues** relating to business. For example, **Big Data**, **outsourcing**, **customer relationship systems** and new methods of **marketing**.
Analysis of scenarios	When reading through any scenario, you need to **think widely** about the issues the organisation faces and how it is **operating** and needs to operate.

All OTQs in all the exams are worth the same number of marks, both in this Kit and in the real exam. However this is an approximate guide: some OTQs are very short and just require a factual selection, which you either know or you don't, while others are more complex, which will inevitably take more time. Note that the real exam will be balanced such that the 'difficulty' of the exam will be fair for all students – the OTQs in this Kit have also been balanced in a similar way.

Using the solutions and feedback

Avoid looking at the answer until you have finished a question. It can be very tempting to do so, but unless you give the question a proper attempt under exam conditions you will not know how you would have coped with it in the real exam scenario.

When you do look at the answer, compare it with your own and give some thought to why your answer was different, if it was.

If you did not reach the correct answer make sure that you work through the explanation or workings provided, to see where you went wrong. If you think that you do not understand the principle involved, work through and revise the point again, to ensure that you will understand it if it occurs in the exam.

Objective test questions

1 Organisational structures

1.1 Romulus Co and Remus Co have recently agreed to co-operate to exploit the possibilities that both companies have in a particular overseas market. No separate company has been established for this purpose as the companies' chief executives, who have known each other for many years, have agreed matters informally.

This arrangement is an example of a:

- ☐ Licensing agreement
- ☐ Joint venture
- ☐ Strategic alliance
- ☐ Outsourcing agreement

1.2 Organisations can be defined or described in various ways.

Which THREE of the following are the key characteristics that are shared by all organisations?

- ☐ Synergy
- ☐ Social arrangement
- ☐ Collective goals
- ☐ Specialisation
- ☐ Controlled performance
- ☐ Exchange of goods and services

1.3 **What are the primary objectives of profit-oriented and non-profit oriented organisations?**

- ☐ Profit-oriented organisation
  Output of goods/services
  Non-profit oriented organisation
  Minimise costs

- ☐ Profit-oriented organisation
  Output of goods/services
  Non-profit oriented organisation
  Provision of goods/services

- ☐ Profit-oriented organisation
  Maximisation of wealth
  Non-profit oriented organisation
  Minimise costs

- ☐ Profit-oriented organisation
  Maximisation of wealth
  Non-profit oriented organisation
  Provision of goods/services

1.4 **Match the terms in the list below to the relevant action by an organisation:**

- Backwards vertical integration
- Horizontal integration
- Forwards vertical integration
- Shared service centre

Term	Action
☐	A company that makes toothbrushes decides to buy a toothpaste company.
☐	Bixons Co, a retailer of electronic devices decides to buy NoxConn Co, which owns and runs a string of electronic device factories in the far east.
☐	A multinational is considering how it does IT support internally. The IT department in one of its locations is so good the company decides to shut down all its other IT departments. It will give greater funding to the single IT department, so it can help the whole company.
☐	A company decides to buy the retail company it has traditionally sold its goods to.

1.5 **Which of the following is the objective of efficient and effective business processes?**

☐ Creating the maximum output
☐ Creating value for money products
☐ Creating the maximum output for minimum input
☐ Creating the best quality output from the available inputs

1.6 A major airline, FlotAir Co, has been drawing up a mission statement.

Which THREE of the following items would you expect to see in it?

☐ We will double profits in three years
☐ We will encourage diversity in the workplace
☐ We intend to be the best airline in the world
☐ We aim to give excellent customer service
☐ We intend to take over Lufthansa
☐ We intend to have a 30% market share on the London to New York route

1.7 The following diagram is of Henry Mintzberg's organisational configuration framework.

Complete the diagram by placing FOUR terms from the list below into the correct position.

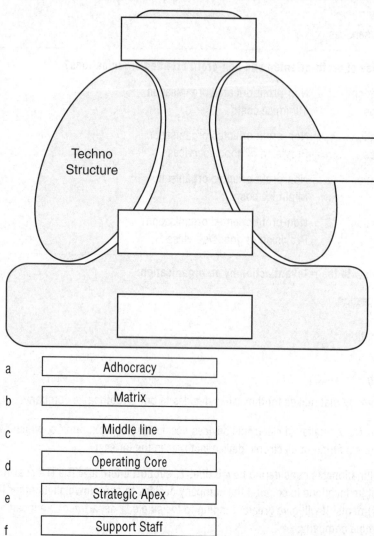

a   Adhocracy

b   Matrix

c   Middle line

d   Operating Core

e   Strategic Apex

f   Support Staff

1.8 A beef burger factory is considering the purchase of its meat supplier.

Acquiring the meat supplier would be:

☐ Horizontal integration
☐ Forwards vertical integration
☐ Backwards vertical integration
☐ Business process outsourcing

1.9 **What does the system boundary separate?**

☐ Individual sub-systems within a system
☐ Input and output devices from the central processor
☐ The system and its components from its environment
☐ The components of a system, allowing them to work independently

1.10 **Which of the following features would NOT normally be associated with a Non-Governmental Organisation (NGO)?**

☐ Government funded
☐ Independent
☐ Non-profit making
☐ Explicit social mission

1.11 **In order to establish whether a particular organisation should be classified as a business or not, it would be necessary to enquire as to the nature of its:**

☐ Primary objective
☐ Mission
☐ Vision
☐ Secondary objective

1.12 **Which of the following characteristics is NOT normally associated with a Non-Governmental Organisation (NGO)?**

☐ Furthering humanitarian causes
☐ Championing social causes
☐ Making profits
☐ Exercising independence

1.13 **Which of the following is NOT a contextual dimension influencing organisational design according to Daft?**

☐ Culture and formalisation
☐ Environment
☐ Geographical dispersion
☐ Technology

1.14 **Which type of systems thinking is used where an organisation introduces new activities to seize marketing opportunities that present themselves in the environment?**

☐ Open
☐ Closed
☐ Decoupling
☐ Entropy

1.15 **Which of the following organisational structures encourages employee flexibility and multiple reporting?**

- ☐ Matrix
- ☐ Centralised
- ☐ Functional
- ☐ Divisional

1.16 **Mintzberg's design of an effective organisation does NOT include which of the following categories?**

- ☐ Technostructure
- ☐ Outsource partners
- ☐ Operating core
- ☐ Strategic apex

1.17 **Which of the following is the primary financial objective of public sector organisations?**

- ☐ Profitability
- ☐ Efficient use of resources
- ☐ Avoidance of loss
- ☐ Maximisation of charitable donations

1.18 **Which of the following is a not-for-profit organisation?**

- ☐ Sole traders
- ☐ Partnerships
- ☐ Mutual organisations
- ☐ Public limited companies

2 Corporate governance and regulation

2.1 **If a government has a macro-economic policy objective of expanding the overall level of economic activity, which of the following measures would NOT be consistent with such an objective?**

- ☐ Increasing public expenditure
- ☐ Lowering interest rates
- ☐ Increasing taxation
- ☐ Decreasing taxation

2.2 **A company may seek to improve corporate governance by ensuring that:**

- ☐ The chairman and chief executive are the same individual in order to avoid confusion over who has responsibility for running the company

- ☐ The chairman and chief executive are different individuals in order to prevent one person having too much power within the company

- ☐ The chairman and chief executive are different individuals in case one dies or becomes incapacitated due to ill health

- ☐ The company chairman does not take up outside directorships

2.3 **Match the terms in the list below to the relevant action:**

- Corporate political activity
- Bridging
- Buffering

Term	Action
[ ]	A housing charity offers to send a senior management team member to a government department to discuss the impact of proposed new squatting laws
[ ]	Salco prides itself in being involved in the political process
[ ]	Erin, an employee of Ertbank, has a defined role in monitoring upcoming legislation that will affect the bank's operation

2.4 **According to Carroll and Buchholtz, a company that was trying to avoid tax, by employing loopholes in the law, could defend its actions by claiming it was engaged in which layer of corporate social responsibility?**

- ☐ Economic
- ☐ Legal
- ☐ Ethical
- ☐ Philanthropic

2.5 Justin Co has a major stakeholder who in the past has been able to exert considerable influence over the environmental impact of the company's manufacturing operations. Specifically, as a result of one recent campaign orchestrated by this stakeholder, a production facility was temporarily closed down for three weeks. The stakeholder writes regularly to the company's chairman regarding a range of environmental issues surrounding the company.

In terms of Mendelow's Matrix the company would be advised to pursue which of the following strategies in respect of this stakeholder?

- ☐ Keep this stakeholder informed at all times about the company
- ☐ Keep this stakeholder satisfied with regard to the company and its strategies
- ☐ Take minimum effort with regard to this stakeholder as they always complain
- ☐ Treat this stakeholder as a key player when formulating future strategies

2.6 **Which of the following is normally subject to the most direct government regulation?**

- ☐ Employment protection
- ☐ Corporate social responsibility
- ☐ Business ethics
- ☐ Corporate governance

2.7 **Anti-monopoly laws are based on the proposition that the best way to achieve efficiency and the avoidance of excessive prices is through:**

- ☐ Regulation
- ☐ Increased competition
- ☐ Public ownership
- ☐ Oligopoly

2.8 **Which of the following corporate social responsibility policies of an organisation is an example of enlightened self-interest?**

☐ The achievement of legal compliance
☐ The achievement of sustainability
☐ The achievement of changes to society and the market
☐ The achievement of best practice

2.9 **Which of the following are examples of conflict between an organisation's stakeholders caused by differences in their aims and objectives?**

Select ALL that apply.

☐ Long-term projects may be prevented by managerial short-termism

☐ Owners of small businesses may lose control of the organisation when it grows and it is necessary to appoint managers to run the business

☐ Mass marketing campaigns may require an increase in the quality of products produced

☐ The financial independence of an organisation may be reduced when additional shares or loans are required

☐ Staffing levels are increased as a consequence of increased capital investment

2.10 Two of Sunshine Tours Co's stakeholder groups are putting the company under pressure to improve its return on investment.

These are most likely to comprise which TWO of the following groups?

☐ Shareholders
☐ Customers
☐ Bankers
☐ Suppliers
☐ Employees

2.11 **Which of the following would be identified as a problem with the role of non-executive director?**

☐ External stakeholder security
☐ Time available to devote to the role
☐ Objective viewpoint
☐ Dual nature as full board members and strong, independent element

2.12 **Which of the following is consistent with a government's policy objective to expand the level of economic activity?**

☐ An increase in taxation
☐ An increase in interest rates
☐ An increase in personal savings
☐ An increase in public expenditure

2.13 **Which of the following has become an established best practice in corporate governance in recent years?**

☐ An increasingly prominent role for non-executive directors
☐ An increase in the powers of external auditors
☐ Greater accountability for directors who are in breach of their fiduciary duties
☐ A requirement for all companies to establish an internal audit function

2.14 **Which of the following is NOT a benefit of corporate governance?**

☐ Improved access to capital markets
☐ Stimulation of performance
☐ Enhanced marketability of goods and services
☐ Prevention of fraudulent claims by contractors

2.15 **The system of policies by which an organisation is directed and controlled is known as which of the following?**

☐ Corporate governance
☐ Corporate social responsibility
☐ Corporate infrastructure
☐ Corporate strategic apex

2.16 **Which of the following is NOT a macroeconomic factor?**

☐ The relationship between price and demand in a particular market
☐ Price inflation
☐ Levels of savings and investment
☐ Unemployment amongst young people

2.17 **Which of the following statements concerning a written code of ethics is correct?**

☐ It sets out the company's attitude to risk
☐ It should be independent of management actions
☐ It supports non-compliance
☐ It is based on the law

2.18 **Having responsible, community-based business practices is an example of which of Caroll and Buchholtz's 'layers of corporate social responsibility'?**

☐ Economic responsibilities
☐ Legal responsibilities
☐ Ethical responsibilities
☐ Philanthropic responsibilities

3 The finance function

3.1 Hayley Porter is an accountant with Worricker Co. Hayley was recently asked to join a project team looking into the strategic position of Worricker Co by considering a range of information from internal and external sources and including financial and non-financial information.

It appears, therefore, that she has been recruited into this project team in order to exploit her expertise in:

☐ Financial reporting
☐ Investment appraisal
☐ Capital budgeting
☐ Strategic management accounting

3.2   The central bank has announced a 2% increase in interest rates.

This decision has the most direct impact on which department of a large company?

- ☐   Marketing
- ☐   Treasury
- ☐   Financial accounting
- ☐   Production

3.3   **Which section of a company's finance function would have primary responsibility for ensuring the sound stewardship by managers of the resources entrusted to them?**

- ☐   The financial transactions recording section
- ☐   The management accounting section
- ☐   The financial reporting section
- ☐   The treasury management section

3.4   Tim Ogube is advising the managing director of Boiled Sweets Co of the advantages of setting standards and targets to specify the levels of performance that underpin the company's control system.

Which THREE of the following are the main components of the company's control system?

- ☐   Measurement of actual performance and comparison against targets
- ☐   Identification of deviations from the plan
- ☐   Establishment of standards or targets to express planned performance
- ☐   Follow-up action to correct adverse results or to exploit favourable variances
- ☐   Measurement of ideal performance
- ☐   Devising the plan

3.5   **When a company's accounting and finance function prepares financial statements in accordance with legal rules and accounting standards, it is engaged in the support activity of:**

- ☐   Record-keeping and stewardship
- ☐   Planning and control
- ☐   External reporting
- ☐   Internal reporting

3.6   **In a typical finance function, preparation of budgets and budgetary control would usually be the responsibility of which of the following roles?**

- ☐   The Financial Accountant
- ☐   The Management Accountant
- ☐   The Treasurer
- ☐   The Finance Director

3.7   Harold is an accountant with Farnworth Co. He was recently asked to join a project team looking into the company's compliance with both FRC and IASB accounting standards.

It appears, therefore, that Harold has been recruited into this project team in order to exploit his expertise in:

- ☐   Financial reporting
- ☐   Performance measurement
- ☐   Capital budgeting
- ☐   Strategic management accounting

3.8 **Identify FOUR ways that the finance function supports a company's corporate objectives?**

- ☐ Maintaining quality controls over finished products
- ☐ Providing shareholders with information
- ☐ Ensuring that sales revenue meets budget
- ☐ Providing management with information
- ☐ Ensuring sufficient availability of inventory
- ☐ Maintaining production capacity
- ☐ Ensuring the availability of working capital
- ☐ Providing information to stakeholders

3.9 **Which THREE of the following are functions associated with treasury management?**

- ☐ Arranging finance
- ☐ Analysis of operating variances
- ☐ Administrating corporate tax affairs
- ☐ Analysis of financial accounting ratios
- ☐ Revaluation of company assets
- ☐ Management of foreign currency holdings

3.10 **Which of the following is NOT an advantage of having a shared finance service centre?**

- ☐ Tailored response
- ☐ Economies of scale
- ☐ Reduction in cost
- ☐ Better quality service

3.11 **Which of the following is a potential consequence of an organisation fraudulently understating its results?**

- ☐ Excessive distribution of profits to shareholders
- ☐ Restricted access to loan finance
- ☐ Unrealistic expectations in the financial markets
- ☐ Potential shortfalls in working capital

3.12 **In order to establish an effective internal control system that will minimise the prospect of fraud, which of the following should be considered first?**

- ☐ Recruitment policy and checks on new personnel
- ☐ Identification of areas of potential risk
- ☐ Devising of appropriate sanctions for inappropriate behaviour
- ☐ Segregation of duties in critical areas

3.13 Collinson Co is a medium-sized group operating at four locations in the UK. It operates an entirely centralised finance function but is concerned that the function as a whole is not performing well.

In which area is centralisation of the finance function least likely to be effective in this situation?

- ☐ External reporting
- ☐ Recording financial transactions
- ☐ Cash management
- ☐ Internal reporting

3.14   **Which THREE of the following are common purposes of budgets?**

☐   Guiding managers on how to achieve company objectives
☐   Supporting the production of a statement of cash flows
☐   Helping to co-ordinate financial reporting activities
☐   Allocating finite company resources
☐   Communicating a company's plans

3.15   **Are the following statements true or false?**

	True	False
All variances should be investigated	☐	☐
Variances are only possible after budgeting	☐	☐
Budgets help to identify the need for a loan	☐	☐
Budgets are made by the treasury function	☐	☐

3.16   **Which of the following statements are incorrect?**

(i)   Inventory reports help to highlight opportunity cost
(ii)   Budgets are required to be included in the financial statements
(iii)   One of the main aims of the finance function is to enable informed decision-making
(iv)   Budgets must be produced at least every half year

☐   (i) only
☐   (ii) and (iv)
☐   (i), (ii) and (iv)
☐   (iii) only

3.17   X Company has shareholders' funds of $125,000. The board has decided that the maximum gearing ratio should be 20%.

Given this constraint, what is the most X Company can borrow?

☐ $104,000
☐ $150,000
☐ $625,000
☐ $25,000

3.18   **According to the independent business partner model, the role of the finance function is to:**

☐   Add value
☐   Create value
☐   Eliminate costs
☐   Prevent fraud

4 The technology and information function

4.1   **When an organisation securely shares part of its private network with customers or other outside parties it is said to operate:**

☐   An internet
☐   An intranet
☐   An extranet
☐   A joint venture

4.2 Information that takes the form of a list of debtors and creditors is by nature said to be:

- ☐ Strategic
- ☐ Tactical
- ☐ Operational
- ☐ Executive

4.3 Technology which encourages user contributions and interactivity is known as:

- ☐ Web 2.0
- ☐ Business 2 Consumer (B2C)
- ☐ E-commerce
- ☐ Teleworking

4.4 Which of the following is NOT an advantage that virtual companies have?

- ☐ Materials can be acquired more cheaply
- ☐ It can respond to the environment quickly
- ☐ It has a low cost base
- ☐ It has a single supply chain

4.5 AggraCo has a supercomputer on site. This computer is capable of a great deal of work. AggraCo has connected the computer to the internet. It has started charging companies who wish to do scientific analysis for use of the supercomputer by the minute. Companies find this agreeable as their typical usage doesn't justify owning a supercomputer. They put complex inputs into the supercomputer, which comes up with an easy to understand output.

This arrangement is best described as:

- ☐ Cloud service
- ☐ WAN
- ☐ Expert system
- ☐ Grid computing

4.6 The main advantages of a database include:

- ☐ The development of separate data sources.
- ☐ Unlimited access and open communication.
- ☐ End user flexibility and devolution of responsibility.
- ☐ Data integrity and elimination of duplication.

4.7 Electronic Executive Information Systems (EIS) and Expert Systems (ES) are examples of:

- ☐ Customer relationship management software
- ☐ Database management systems
- ☐ Computer networking
- ☐ Decision-based software

4.8 Regular reporting on stockholding of products (inventory) is an example of which level of organisational information?

- ☐ Strategic
- ☐ Tactical
- ☐ Integrative
- ☐ Techno-structural

4.9 Which of the following describes how introducing information technology can enhance business processes?

☐ Increasing the length of existing processes
☐ Redirecting existing information flows
☐ Replacing inefficient parallel processes with efficient sequential processes
☐ Reducing delays in the decision making of management

4.10 Match the architecture in the list below to the relevant description.

- Tree
- Mesh
- Star
- Bus

Architecture	Description
	All computers in the company can communicate directly with one another through a number of possible routes.
	A central cable or spine exists, through which all computers in the company communicate.
	A central server is connected to all computers and helps them communicate.
	A central server is connected to a number of other servers, and these servers each have a collection of computers attached to them.

4.11 Which of the following is most likely to lead to an organisation accessing a larger market for its goods or services?

☐ Electronic Data Interchange (EDI)
☐ Teleworking
☐ E-commerce
☐ Penetration marketing

4.12 Dispersed and virtual teams are normally a result of:

☐ An economic downturn
☐ Developments in technology and information systems
☐ Poor staff morale and motivation within the workforce
☐ Ineffective human resourcing practices

4.13 Integrated solutions in product design and control of machinery are based on:

☐ A shared customer focused outlook
☐ A JIT philosophy
☐ CAD and CAM technologies
☐ Decision support systems

4.14 A software management system combining all of a globally diverse organisation's sales, marketing and customer support information is known as:

☐ Distributed data processing (DDP)
☐ Customer relationship management (CRM)
☐ A database management system (DBMS)
☐ A wide area network (WAN)

4.15 **A system that simulates the problem solving techniques of human experts is known as:**

- ☐ An expert system
- ☐ A knowledge transfer programme
- ☐ A smart system
- ☐ A management information system

4.16 **Which of the following is a system that enables a business to manage its relationships centrally through the storage of existing and potential customer contact information, accounts and leads?**

- ☐ Customer relationship management system
- ☐ Expert system
- ☐ E-commerce
- ☐ Cloud computing

4.17 **Regular reporting on stockholding of products (inventory) is an example of which level of organisational information?**

- ☐ Strategic
- ☐ Tactical
- ☐ Integrative
- ☐ Techno-structural

4.18 **Which of the following statements concerning Big Data analytics is correct?**

- ☐ Big Data analytics relies on digital information
- ☐ Big Data analytics relies on written information
- ☐ Big Data analytics relies on verbal information
- ☐ Big Data analytics relies on confidential information

5 System implementation and business strategy

5.1 **The technique of force field analysis depicts:**

- ☐ Change as occurring through a series of restraining and driving forces.
- ☐ Growth of organisations through evolution and revolution.
- ☐ An organisation's environment as a series of opportunistic and threatening factors.
- ☐ Aggressive management styles used to drive change.

5.2 **Which of the following is NOT normally associated with outsourced IS solutions?**

- ☐ Ensuring contract compliance
- ☐ Assembly and maintenance of a suitably skilled workforce
- ☐ Preparing formal tendering documents
- ☐ Invoicing, processing and payment

5.3 **Which of Kotter and Schlesinger's methods of dealing with resistance to change would result in awarding generous redundancy packages to employees who lose out as a result of the change?**

- ☐ Facilitation and support
- ☐ Negotiation and agreement
- ☐ Manipulation and co-optation
- ☐ Explicit and implicit coercion

5.4 A data input clerk comes across an on screen error message stating that a field is incomplete. They will not be allowed to move from this screen until the field is complete.

This is an example of:

☐ An application control
☐ A general control
☐ Implicit control

5.5 A main aim of electronic data interchange (EDI) is:

☐ To improve communication exchanges within an organisation
☐ To replace conventional documentation with structured electronically transmitted data
☐ To allow employees to work at home
☐ To create a shared data resource within an organisation

5.6 ABC sells mobile telephones. Each phone sold is supplied with a charger, earpiece, car charger and other accessories which can only be used with ABC Co phones. Its predictive text style is also very different to that of other manufacturers.

To which of Porter's five forces is this strategy intended to respond?

☐ Bargaining power of suppliers
☐ Bargaining power of customers
☐ Threat of new entrants
☐ Intensity of competitive rivalry

5.7 Service Level Agreements are normally associated with:

☐ Job reductions negotiated with staff groups
☐ Deskilling
☐ Agreed appraisal outcomes
☐ Outsourcing

5.8 Which TWO of the following are advantages of using a modular changeover method of implementation?

☐ Less risky than direct
☐ Minimises workload
☐ Problems are likely to be in one area
☐ Minimises cost
☐ Provides a way of verifying results

5.9 Std Co offers payroll services to a number of organisations.

Which level of service provision is this?

☐ Facilities management
☐ Timeshare
☐ Service bureaux
☐ Multiple sourcing

5.10 Which of the following does NOT represent a control in a computer network?

☐ A firewall
☐ Data encryption
☐ Passwords
☐ A cookie

5.11 According to Kurt Lewin, the final stage of his three stage model of change is called:

- ☐ Unfreezing
- ☐ Refreezing
- ☐ Unbundling
- ☐ Support and facilitation

5.12 One possible response to change is regressive or non-learning behaviour, which is also termed:

- ☐ Passive resistance
- ☐ Passive resignation
- ☐ Active resistance
- ☐ Active resignation

5.13 M Co has decided to outsource its IT support to N Co.

Which of the following are DISADVANTAGES to M Co as a result of this decision?

1   M Co becomes a more complex organisation.
2   Urgent IT issues at M Co may not be resolved as quickly.
3   Ongoing IT costs of M Co will increase.
4   Longer term contracts with N Co are prone to disruption.

- ☐ 1 and 3
- ☐ 2 and 3
- ☐ 1 and 4
- ☐ 2 and 4

5.14 Porter's value system shows the organisation in terms of:

- ☐ The value chains of suppliers, channels and the customer
- ☐ Primary activities, support activities and margin
- ☐ The technostructure, strategic apex and operating core
- ☐ Passive, independent, supportive and integrative approaches to supply

5.15 IS client-vendor relationship is a feature of which of the following?

- ☐ An outsourced IS function
- ☐ Enterprise-wide systems
- ☐ Social networking
- ☐ Virtual team working

5.16 With regard to Porter's Five Forces Analysis and new entrants into a market, which of the following pairs of statements is correct?

- ☐ Encourages new entrants   Erects a barrier to new entrants
  High competition   Low capital costs

- ☐ Encourages new entrants   Erects a barrier to new entrants
  A monopoly supplier of a vital component   High competition

- ☐ Encourages new entrants   Erects a barrier to new entrants
  One large customer   A monopoly supplier of a vital components

- ☐ Encourages new entrants   Erects a barrier to new entrants
  Low competition   High capital costs

5.17 **'Corrective' refers to a type of systems maintenance performed to:**

- ☐ Remedy software defects
- ☐ Allow executive level unstructured decision-making
- ☐ Adjust applications to user preferences
- ☐ Prevent future operation delays

5.18 **Electronic data interchange relies on:**

- ☐ Structured data and standard business documents
- ☐ Networking and creativity
- ☐ Social networking and intelligence sharing
- ☐ A system (or software) development cycle

6 Operations management and the organisation

6.1 **Supply chain partnerships grow out of:**

- ☐ Quality accreditation
- ☐ Recognising the supply chain and linkages in a value system
- ☐ An expansion of trade
- ☐ Adopting a marketing philosophy

6.2 Hairdooz Co operates a large chain of hairdressing salons. Peter, a management consultant, has been asked to undertake a review of the company's activities in providing its services to customers. In terms of Porter's Value Chain, Peter has been asked to focus on the primary activities of the company.

Peter will, therefore, be analysing which THREE of the following?

- ☐ Inbound logistics
- ☐ Procurement
- ☐ Firm infrastructure
- ☐ Marketing and sales
- ☐ Service

6.3 **Porter's value system reflects the value created through the relationship of:**

- ☐ Suppliers, manufacturers, distribution channels and customers' value chains
- ☐ Customers and sales staff
- ☐ Production and sales departments
- ☐ Economy, efficiency and effectiveness in the use of resources

6.4 **Reck and Long's strategic positioning tool measures the contribution of which of the following organisational functions?**

- ☐ Quality control and assurance
- ☐ Purchasing and supply
- ☐ The management of systems
- ☐ The management of human resources

6.5 **Match the terms below to the relevant part of the process for an accounting firm:**

- Transforming inputs
- Transformed inputs
- Outputs
- Transformation process

Term	Process part
	The trained accountant
	The client's transactional data
	The financial statements
	The audit

6.6 **Inbound logistics is:**

☐ A secondary activity that refers to price negotiation of incoming raw materials
☐ A secondary activity that refers to receipt, storage and inward distribution of raw materials
☐ A primary activity that refers to inbound enquiries and customer complaints
☐ A primary activity that refers to receipt, storage and inward distribution of raw materials

---

6.7 **Which of the following measures will help an organisation to limit its enviromental impact?**

1 Recycling waste
2 Using energy efficient electrical appliances
3 Selecting suppliers carefully
4 Buying raw materials locally

☐ 1 and 2 only
☐ 2 and 4 only
☐ 1 and 3 only
☐ 1, 2, 3 and 4

6.8 **Supplier relationships in a supply network are categorised in which of the following ways?**

☐ Single, multiple, delegated and parallel
☐ Primary, secondary and post-purchase
☐ Phased, pilot and integrated
☐ One-to-one, several to one, 180 degrees and 360 degrees

6.9 **Which of the following is the main characteristic of a demand network?**

☐ Products are pushed onto the market by the manufacturer
☐ Products are developed in response to market signals
☐ Businesses in the network operate relatively independently
☐ Interdependence of channel members is reduced

6.10 **Which of the following is NOT one of the four Vs used to analyse the differences between transformational processes?**

☐ Volume
☐ Variety
☐ Velocity
☐ Visibility

6.11 **In purchasing, the 'Reck and Long' positioning tool is by nature:**

☐ Strategic
☐ Independent
☐ Supportive
☐ Passive

6.12 BCD Co is a large trading company. Steve is the administration manager and is also responsible for legal and compliance functions. Sheila is responsible for after sales service and has responsibility for ensuring that customers who have purchased goods from BCD Co are fully satisfied. Sunny deals with suppliers and negotiates on the price and quality of inventory. He is also responsible for identifying the most appropriate suppliers of plant and machinery for the factory. Sam is the information technology manager and is responsible for all information systems within the company.

According to Porter's value chain, which of the managers is involved in a primary activity?

☐ Steve
☐ Sheila
☐ Sunny
☐ Sam

16.13 Porter's five forces model identifies factors which determine the nature and strength of competition in an industry.

Which of the following is NOT one of the five forces identified in Porter's model?

☐ Substitute products or services
☐ New entrants to the industry
☐ Bargaining power of customers
☐ Government regulation of the industry

6.14 **Most supply chains involve which of the following?**

☐ A number of different companies
☐ An organisation's infrastructure
☐ After sales service
☐ A strategic apex

6.15 **Which of the following best describes 'benchmarking'?**

☐ Setting and monitoring internal performance standards
☐ Comparison of actual production against budgeted production
☐ Comparison of a service, practice or process against one or more similar activities
☐ Setting a mission statement and ensuring that statement is met over time

6.16   Reck and Long devised a model that aimed to provide an insight into the evolution of the purchasing function.

Match Reck and Long's phases from the list below to the relevant characteristic:

- Independent
- Integrative
- Passive
- Supportive

Phase   *Characteristic*

| | Purchasing reacts to requests from other departments |

| | Recognition that negotiation with suppliers is important |

| | Emphasis on co-ordination and compliance with centrally negotiated contracts |

| | Suppliers are viewed as partners |

6.17   **Use the words from the list below to complete the following statement:**

- Create
- Fulfill
- Market requirements
- Resources

In operations management [   ] are used to [   ] outputs that [   ] specific [   ]

7 Quality Management

7.1   **Corrective work, the cost of scrap and materials lost are:**

- ☐ Examples of internal failure costs
- ☐ Examples of external failure costs
- ☐ Examples of appraisal costs
- ☐ Examples of preventative costs

7.2   **What aspect of total quality management (TQM) provides for the participation by selected employees in quality improvement, through meetings to discuss quality-related issues?**

- ☐ Work cells
- ☐ Continuous improvement
- ☐ Quality circles
- ☐ Empowerment

7.3   **Approval of documentation, procedures manuals and work instructions is associated with:**

- ☐ Registration under the standards required for quality certification
- ☐ Total quality management (TQM)
- ☐ Lean production methods
- ☐ Job evaluation

7.4 **Which of the following measures customer, operational and financial aspects of quality?**

☐ SERVQUAL
☐ Balanced scorecards
☐ Value for money audits
☐ Total quality management

7.5 **Total productive maintenance involves:**

☐ Maintaining worker satisfaction and high productivity
☐ A cycle of PDCA
☐ A prevention of quality failures through equipment faults
☐ Eliminating non-value adding activities from a process

7.6 **The technique PDCA represents:**

☐ A programme development control activity used in information management
☐ A framework for bringing about quality improvement to a process or system
☐ A software inventory system used in warehouse management
☐ People, developments, controls and appraisal in strategic human resourcing

7.7 **What category of quality cost is a cost arising from inadequate quality, where the problem is identified before a finished product or service is delivered to the external customer?**

☐ Internal failure cost
☐ External failure cost
☐ Appraisal cost
☐ Inspection cost

7.8 **Gaining International Standards (ISO) in quality is mainly dependent upon:**

☐ Effective processes for documentation and control
☐ A shared quality philosophy
☐ Commitment from middle managers
☐ Benchmarking customer related performance against competitors

7.9 **A necessary product/service requirement to meet the Japanese interpretation of 'quality' is:**

☐ To comply with all safety standards
☐ To cost no more than necessary
☐ To meet a design brief
☐ To meet customer expectations

7.10 **Servqual relies on feedback from:**

☐ Customers
☐ Managers
☐ Careful business process re-engineering
☐ A 360 degree appraisal

7.11 What is 'Theory Z'?

☐ An addition to McGregor's motivation theory.

☐ The application of Japanese managerial practices into Western culture.

☐ An explanation of how the attainment of career paths by individuals results in lack of association with a specific company.

☐ The last theory produced by Maslow, relating to the application of hygiene factors to the Japanese model of lean production.

7.12 The 5-S model refers to:

☐ Internal analysis involving structure, sub-structure, systems, sub-systems and strategy.
☐ Internal analysis involving style, shared values, skills, staffing and 'soft' information.
☐ Operations management practices of structurise, systematise, sanitise, standardise and self-discipline.
☐ The Japanese six-sigma model adapted to Western practice.

7.13 Gaining International Standards (ISO) in quality is mainly dependent upon:

☐ Effective processes for documentation and control
☐ A shared quality philosophy
☐ Commitment from middle managers
☐ Benchmarking customer related performance against competitors

7.14 A manufacturer concerned mainly with production efficiencies and reducing unit costs is known as:

☐ Product oriented
☐ Production oriented
☐ Operationally strategic
☐ A learning organisation

7.15 Which of the following is NOT associated with quality management?

☐ 5-S practice
☐ 180 degree feedback
☐ Six Sigma methodology
☐ Five-why process

7.16 Critical service quality factors include all but which of the following?

☐ Responsiveness
☐ Integrity
☐ Communication
☐ Competence

8 Managing capacity and inventory

8.1 Which of the following describes the ABC system of inventory control?

☐ A Japanese-style problem solving device that is particularly helpful in inventory management.
☐ An inventory management method that concentrates effort on the most important items.
☐ Accuracy, brevity and clarity in the quality of system reporting.
☐ A manual solution to managing inventory.

8.2 **In which type of production layout do people, materials and other resources travel to the product being produced?**

- ☐ Product
- ☐ Cell
- ☐ Fixed
- ☐ Process

8.3 Howell Co's procurement manager Patrick is deciding on the quantity of a new material, Ubbo, to order in preparation for production of a major new product.

To do so he needs to balance:

- ☐ The risk of delay in production caused by insufficient Ubbo against the risk of the Ubbo quality being poor.

- ☐ The risk of delay in production against the cost of holding inventory of Ubbo.

- ☐ The current price of Ubbo against the risk of it rising.

- ☐ The current price of Ubbo against the lead time of delivery.

8.4 **Inventory management using a method that concentrates effort on the most expensive items is called:**

- ☐ PDCA
- ☐ JIT
- ☐ Five S
- ☐ ABC

8.5 Babbage Co enters designs into a computer. The computer controls a cutting arm that cuts shapes into metal. Babbage staff then assemble the shapes into electrical devices.

Babbage is making good use of:

- ☐ Robots
- ☐ Computer numerical control
- ☐ Decision support systems
- ☐ Enterprise resource systems

8.6 **Which of the following is an approach of producing goods or purchasing inventory only when required?**

- ☐ Just-in-time
- ☐ Ad hoc
- ☐ Level capacity strategy
- ☐ Plan-do-check-act (PDCA) quality

8.7 **Which of the following describes what EOQ is?**

- ☐ Inventory system based on economic order quantities
- ☐ European observance quality certification
- ☐ Equal opportunity quantification index used in HRM
- ☐ Japanese-inspired technique aimed at continuous improvement

8.8 Laramy Co is a small factory specialising in garden furniture. It places a high value on teams. Each of its highly trained 5 person teams can create a product from raw materials. Wood and other materials are received, and the team transforms them into Laramy's product lines.

Which flow setup is this?

☐ Process

☐ Cell

☐ Product

☐ Fixed

8.9 **Which of the following is a feature of a fixed position production layout?**

☐ There is little movement of plant and staff.

☐ A high variety of tasks are performed in one place.

☐ There will be restrictions on quality testing.

☐ There are high unit costs.

8.10 **Which TWO of the following would typically NOT be used as process technology?**

☐ Computer numerical control

☐ Flexible manufacturing system

☐ Automated guided vehicles

☐ Customer relationship management system

☐ Expert system

☐ Big Data

8.11 **Which of the following best describes the ABC inventory management system?**

☐ Monitors inventory levels, so when these drop below a critical level, more inventory is ordered

☐ Requires that inventory is counted on a regular basis (perhaps every week) and re-ordered as necessary

☐ Focuses inventory management on the 20% of items (representing 80% of inventory expenditure) which need careful monitoring

☐ Identifies the amount of buffer stock required to ensure that stockouts are kept to a minimum

---

8.12 **Which of the following describes a chase demand plan?**

☐ Activity is adjusted depending upon demand.

☐ Activity is maintained at maximum levels.

☐ Activity is maintained at minimum levels.

☐ Activity is maintained at a constant level regardless of demand.

8.13 **Optimised production technologies (OPT) is an operations management system which aims to:**

☐ Improve distribution networks

☐ Improve supply sourcing alternatives

☐ Integrate operations and quality assurance

☐ Reduce production bottlenecks

9 The marketing concept

9.1 Why do marketers often segment a market?

☐ To allow marketing staff to allocate their workload fairly
☐ Because most markets are too large to sell to everyone
☐ Because it is well-established best practice
☐ Because customers that share certain characteristics are likely to exhibit similar buying behaviour

9.2 Undifferentiated market positioning involves the targeting of:

☐ A single market segment with a single marketing mix
☐ A single market segment ignoring the concept of the marketing mix
☐ An entire market with a different marketing mix for each segment
☐ An entire market with a single marketing mix

9.3 An organisational approach that involves targeting an entire market with a single marketing mix is known as which of the following?

☐ Undifferentiated
☐ Differentiated
☐ Saturated
☐ Blanket

9.4 Which of the following is the most cost-effective base for market segmentation?

☐ Behavioural
☐ Psychological
☐ Geo-demographic
☐ Demographic

9.5 Which of the following is a type of marketing that involves identifying the markets the organisation should operate in?

☐ Mass marketing
☐ Target marketing
☐ Strategic marketing
☐ Tactical marketing

9.6 Organisations that focus primarily on product features are said to be:

☐ Sales oriented
☐ Product orientated
☐ Market orientated
☐ Production orientated

9.7 In terms of market positioning, concentrated positioning means to:

☐ Target a single market segment with a specific product
☐ Target the whole market with a single product
☐ Target each market segment with a distinct marketing mix
☐ Target a single market with a range of products

9.8 A company that concentrates on product features it instinctively believes to be 'right' is referred to as:

- ☐ A learning organisation
- ☐ Production orientated
- ☐ Product orientated
- ☐ Early stage entrepreneurial

9.9 Which of the following describes an aspect of marketing rather than selling?

- ☐ It is concerned with meeting customers' needs for value in the delivery process
- ☐ Customer design is of low importance
- ☐ It is concerned with the satisfaction of customer needs over the long term
- ☐ The stimulation of demand is of low importance

9.10 'Push' promotion polices involve:

- ☐ High levels of promotional expenditure to encourage consumers to purchase products
- ☐ Transferring finished goods to intermediaries who then have the task of selling those goods to consumers
- ☐ Using different promotional techniques to influence customer demand in different market segments
- ☐ Using just in time supply policies to meet customer demand

9.11 Which of the following is NOT a base for demographic segmentation?

- ☐ Family lifecycle stage
- ☐ Gender
- ☐ Age
- ☐ Education

9.12 Which of the following statements best represents 'a marketing orientation'?

- ☐ Support for the marketing department from top management
- ☐ A large marketing budget
- ☐ High profile advertising campaigns
- ☐ A focus on customer needs

9.13 Which of the following would raise ethical issues for a manufacturer of fast-moving consumer goods?

- (i)   The materials used in manufacture of the goods
- (ii)   The quality of the goods
- (iii) How the goods are advertised
- (iv) How much its raw materials suppliers pay their staff
- (v)   How the goods are packaged

- ☐ (ii) and (iii) only
- ☐ (i), (ii) and (iii) only
- ☐ (ii), (iii) and (v) only
- ☐ (i), (ii), (iii), (iv) and (v)

9.14 For organisations failing to adopt the marketing philosophy, which of the following is NOT recognised as an alternative?

- ☐ Sales orientation
- ☐ Product orientation
- ☐ Lean orientation
- ☐ Production orientation

9.15 Distribution channels, transport, warehouse and sales outlet locations are all examples of:

☐ 'Place', one component of the marketing mix
☐ 'Promotion', one component of the marketing mix
☐ 'Physical evidence', one component of the marketing mix
☐ The management of operations for a service organisation

9.16 Effective product promotion is centred on:

☐ Production processes
☐ Customers and communication
☐ Bonuses for sales staff and product quality
☐ Effective systems of monitoring and control

10 Marketing techniques

10.1 A pricing policy designed to establish or increase market share is referred to as:

☐ Penetration pricing
☐ Skim pricing
☐ Cost-plus pricing
☐ Market leader pricing

10.2 Which of the following shows the correct stages and sequence of the product life cycle?

☐ Product, price, promotion, place
☐ Introduction, growth, maturity, decline
☐ Introduction, growth, middle-age, maturity, decline
☐ Product, price, promotion, place, people

10.3 Direct mailing, branding activities and public relations campaigns are all examples of:

☐ Market process
☐ Product placement
☐ Promotion
☐ Market research

10.4 The Zulon product is manufactured by Arto Co. The product manager for the Zulon is pleased that its dominant market share has been maintained for over five years, but is concerned that market growth has now almost ceased. The product manager does not believe that the product is worthy of any further significant financial support.

In these circumstances and in terms of the BCG Matrix, the product manager should be recommending which of the following strategies?

☐ Hold
☐ Harvest
☐ Divest
☐ Build

10.5 Hessehoff is a Scandinavian manufacturer of trekking gear, such as raincoats and boots. It has always left marketing its goods to the outdoor shops that stock its goods. Recently, a trend has developed where customers visiting Hessehoff's country for a walking holiday have included a tour of the factory in their trip. This has often resulted in good sales at high margin, as the retailers are cut out.

The recent trend would most accurately be described as:

☐ Interactive marketing
☐ Guerrilla marketing
☐ Zero level distribution
☐ Business process redesign

10.6 **Charging a very low price on one item in order to generate customer loyalty and increased sales of other items is called:**

☐ Market penetration
☐ Loss leader pricing
☐ Product penetration
☐ Skim pricing

10.7 **The product life cycle is depicted on a chart or diagram as a line against the variables of:**

☐ Cash flow and market share
☐ Number of customers and sales value
☐ Sales volume and time
☐ Relative market share and market growth rate

10.8 **The extended marketing mix does NOT include which of the following?**

☐ People
☐ Processes
☐ Physical evidence
☐ Positioning

10.9 **Which aspect of the promotional mix does post-modern marketing most fit into?**

☐ Personal and interactive
☐ Mass media
☐ Experiential
☐ Personal and direct

10.10 **Which IS/IT system is Big Data most closely related to?**

☐ Customer Relationship Management (CRM)
☐ Transaction Processing System (TPS)
☐ Expert System (ES)
☐ Digital-marketing

10.11 **An approach that encourages individuals to pass on a marketing message through existing social networks is known as:**

☐ Guerrilla marketing.
☐ Viral marketing.
☐ Experiential marketing.
☐ Cause marketing.

10.12 In terms of internet advertising, which of the following may be regarded as an unhelpful feature when attempting to achieve positive brand awareness?

- ☐ The ability to personalise adverts to the user
- ☐ The ability to target consumers in a certain location
- ☐ The provision of games and entertainment as part of the advert
- ☐ Quick and easy ability to provide pop-up advertising on-screen

10.13 Jane is working on an advertising campaign for her new lawyer's firm. She's decided to work on the anxieties of the public. She is putting together an advert where a child experiences worse and worse conditions until eventually living on the street, as a result of its parents' inability to put a proper will in place.

What kind of marketing is Jane doing?

- ☐ Relationship
- ☐ Experiential
- ☐ Post-modern
- ☐ Guerrilla

10.14 Ralph Moren, a fashion house has decided to implement cutting edge IT to support its marketing. It has programmed a robot to search through every image on the internet and through image recognition software highlight users that are in photos wearing Ralph Moren clothes. It then intends to use information about these people to inform its next round of marketing.

What type of marketing is Ralph Moren engaged in?

- ☐ E-marketing
- ☐ Post-modern marketing
- ☐ Relationship marketing
- ☐ Big Data marketing

10.15 'Market shakeout' involves the weakest producers exiting a particular market and occurs in a period between:

- ☐ Growth through creativity and growth through direction
- ☐ Introduction and market growth
- ☐ Market growth and market maturity
- ☐ Market maturity and decline

10.16 Match the concepts listed below to the relevant situation.

- • Big Data
- • An expert system
- • Relationship marketing
- • Post-modern marketing

Concept	Situation
	A website is able to take user inputs about their preferred climate and activities to suggest a perfect holiday
	When a user points their camera-phone at another person, an app shows how a piece of clothing would look on them. Users are encouraged to upload pictures of themselves wearing the virtual clothing, to be used in the company website
	A site is able to read your email, and analyse the photos you attach to your email. It uses this to tailor the adverts it shows you
	A company prides itself on never sending an email to a user without a prompt. Prompts include asking about recent purchases, and how they could improve the service, and making the user aware of a sale on an item they we indicated is a 'favourite'

10.17 **What is 'market skimming'?**

☐ Setting a price based on the cost of the product plus a mark up
☐ Setting different prices for the same product depending on the market segment
☐ Setting a relatively low price for a new product
☐ Setting an initially high price for a new product

11 Developments in marketing

11.1 **In social marketing, goods that society discourages because of their negative social effects are known as:**

☐ Demerit goods
☐ Durable goods
☐ International embargoes
☐ Imports

11.2 **Select which statement(s) is/are true:**

1. A demerit good is one that is illegal
2. A merit good is provided free of charge by the government

☐ 1. True 2. True
☐ 1. True 2. False
☐ 1. False 2. False
☐ 1. False 2. True

11.3 **The opposing segment of the company workforce is likely to force compromise in which TWO of the following areas of the internal marketing mix?**

☐ Product
☐ Price
☐ Place
☐ Promotion

11.4 Sharna is the CEO of a large business consultancy. She has recently had a lot of negative feedback. Her employees were outraged that they now have to wear uniforms in the office and at client visits. Sharna feels she didn't have a chance to explain the initiative and its benefits, since her PA sent a company-wide email detailing the change.

Sharna has failed to consider the following aspect of the internal marketing mix:

☐ Product
☐ Price
☐ Place
☐ Promotion

11.5 Badpigsco is a recruitment agency specialising in finding the right person for the role. The company is actively using social media to connect with its pool of candidates.

Match Kaplan's categories of social media activity in the list below to the relevant activities of the company.

- Individualise
- Involve
- Integrate
- Initiate

Category	Activity
	Badpigsco's website links with a popular social media website to integrate its data with candidate's previous jobs and narrow the search for a suitable job
	Candidates are encouraged to write a blog on the company website about their work placement. A voucher is given to the best entry every month
	Badpigsco publishes an article monthly and invites candidates to discuss the issues raised
	The website has individualised settings that allow a candidate to set the frequency of communications received so as not to become a nuisance

11.6 Yolocorp, a company specialising in youth-films has recently brought out 'Yolo Swaggins'. The product is a figurine of a character in its satirical remake of a popular fantasy film. Yolocorp has always used social media to connect with its audience. It will send a message to those who have 'liked' the film announcing the availability of the figurine. It also intends to give away figurines to customers who 'share' a 'selfie' showing them watching the film.

The activities of Yolocorp would best be described by Kaplan using which TWO of the following?

- ☐ Individualise
- ☐ Involve
- ☐ Integrate
- ☐ Initiate

11.7 Social media may be a particularly good medium for marketing for a particular type of organisation.

Which of the following may find it particularly beneficial?

- ☐ A multinational
- ☐ A company based in another country
- ☐ A small business
- ☐ A limited liability partnership

11.8 Tinyco is a children's sports goods retailer. It recently has had success marketing sports goods depicting graphically violent sports characters to children.

This would be seen as:

- ☐ Ethical and legal
- ☐ Unethical and legal
- ☐ Ethical but illegal
- ☐ Unethical and illegal

11.9 **Which of the following does NOT make internal marketing more difficult?**

☐ Flatter management structures
☐ The 'virtual' organisation
☐ Employer branding
☐ Globalisation

11.10 Frank is considering volunteering on his gap year. After showing an interest his friend told him about a trip he found out about from a magazine involving a charity. The charity has outlined its plans to send a group of gap year students into an emerging country to build an orphanage. The charity has not done a good job putting together its specific marketing mix for a person like Frank. Frank has a number of reservations about the project.

Match the elements of the charity marketing mix below to Frank's concerns.

- Product
- Price
- Place
- Process

Category	Concern
	Frank had to find out about the trip from his friend, not reading the magazine where they advertised
	Frank questions the flight carrier that the charity has chosen to transport the group to the country, arguing that they travel just as well by freight ferry
	Frank has not found it easy to put his information into the charity's website. It keeps rejecting his passport number as he is not a UK national
	Frank does not believe that building an orphanage is as important as helping in a local hospital

---

11.11 **Match the types of marketing listed below to the relevant company activity.**

- Relationship
- Post-modern
- Guerrilla
- Viral

Type of marketing	Activity
	NiffNaff is a mobile phone network that prides itself on taking suggestions from its customers seriously
	Aggracorp has filmed its factory staff singing and dancing in the hope this will be spread on social media
	Partyco organised an impromptu and possibly illegal party on government premises saying it could liven up any location. Press covered it eagerly and the message was spread exponentially
	Winga, a brewer, used the location of customers from their phones to send interesting facts about the neighbourhood. It suggested bars where the customer could order their drinks. Customers would 'collect' these locations for prizes

11.12 **The maximisation of customer retention and satisfaction through two-way communication is known as:**

- ☐ Postmodern marketing
- ☐ Experiential marketing
- ☐ Relationship marketing
- ☐ E-marketing

11.13 'It is essential that efficient back-office procedures and operations are in place that allow the fulfilment of orders placed via a website.'

What does this statement mean?

- ☐ Websites must be hosted on a stable mainframe computer to ensure sufficient capacity

- ☐ Orders received online should be printed out in case of system failure

- ☐ Internet server computers should be situated at the back of the office

- ☐ Accepting orders online is only the first step – the challenge then is to deliver the product or service ordered

12 Human resources management

12.1 **Abraham Maslow's theory of motivation is often represented as:**

- ☐ A hierarchy of needs.
- ☐ Individual behaviour labelled X or Y.
- ☐ A scientific relationship between work and reward.
- ☐ A series of negative and a series of positive factors.

12.2 **Which of the following is the key factor influencing the supply of labour within a local area?**

- ☐ National unemployment levels
- ☐ The number of graduates leaving university with top degrees
- ☐ The closure of another workplace within the vicinity that employs staff with similar skills
- ☐ The availability of industry-wide training schemes

12.3 **Which TWO of the following would NOT be useful in dealing with surplus in the HR plan?**

- ☐ Overtime
- ☐ Natural wastage
- ☐ Restricting recruitment
- ☐ Reducing labour turnover, by reviewing possible causes
- ☐ Introduce part-time working for previously full-time employees
- ☐ Redundancies

12.4 Darlene, a part CIMA qualified analyst, has been asked to replace her manager, who has a tickly cough and feels poorly. Initially Darlene is excited as her manager deals directly with the client, making this a prestigious job and chance to shine. She's realised, however, that her manager was required to run the job as she is fully CIMA qualified. The CEO of the company has told Darlene she worries too much, and should take this opportunity with both hands.

Which TWO CIMA ethical guidelines would Darlene be breaking if she went along with the plan?

- ☐ Integrity
- ☐ Objectivity
- ☐ Professional competence and due care
- ☐ Confidentiality
- ☐ Professional behaviour

12.5 The main weakness of performance related pay is:

☐ There is no attempt to link profits with the pay structure of individuals
☐ If targets are not met then employees may become demotivated
☐ Employees rarely work harder for additional remuneration
☐ It is almost impossible to set appropriate performance targets for manual workers

12.6 Content theories of motivation tend to focus mainly on:

☐ The needs of the group
☐ Feelings of complacency or dissatisfaction
☐ The needs of individuals
☐ The use of 'carrots' and 'sticks' as devices

12.7 Which of the equations below represents Victor Vroom's model of motivation (Force may sometimes be replaced by Motivation in this equation)?

☐ Force × Valence = Expectation
☐ Force × Expectation = Subjective probability
☐ Subjective probability × Expectation = Force
☐ Force = Valence × Expectation

12.8 Motivation theories and reward systems derived from F W Taylor's thinking are by nature best described as:

☐ Behavioural
☐ Human relations
☐ Content
☐ Scientific

12.9 Enlargement, enrichment and rotation are terms associated with which of the following?

☐ Adjustments to an individual's job content and role
☐ Improvements brought about by competitive benchmarking
☐ Market and product development strategies
☐ Customer approval ratings

12.10 Which of the following is unlikely to be a feature of a successful incentive scheme?

☐ Profit sharing
☐ A clear link between performance and reward
☐ Significant influence by uncontrollable factors
☐ Key results are identified and specified in detail

12.11 In the expectancy theory of motivation a person's preference for a particular outcome is referred to as:

☐ A valence
☐ A hygiene factor
☐ A motivator
☐ Preference discrimination

12.12 The unwritten expectations that the organisation and the individual have of each other is referred to as:

☐ A valence
☐ Work/life balance
☐ The psychological contract
☐ Expectation management

12.13 Which of the following describes the psychological contract?

- ☐ The responsibilities of a member of society to their country
- ☐ The mutual expectations of an employee and employer
- ☐ The intangible benefits arising from outsourcing
- ☐ The use of expert systems in the psychometric testing of new recruits

12.14 Which of the following is a DISADVANTAGE of performance related pay?

- ☐ Not all employees receive the same pay rise
- ☐ It motivates employees to improve their performance
- ☐ It rewards good performance
- ☐ It requires close monitoring of relationships and performance and therefore has a cost

12.15 Which of the following is NOT a valid outcome of a Human Resource Management strategy?

- ☐ Financial outcomes
- ☐ Behavioural outcomes
- ☐ Performance outcomes
- ☐ Process outcomes

12.16 Which of the following is an example of human resource management rather than personnel management?

- ☐ Priority is given to the needs of the employees
- ☐ Employees are considered as a resource to be controlled
- ☐ Strong and regular communication to and from the workforce
- ☐ Priority is given to funding employee pension schemes

13 Human resources practices

13.1 An 'assessment centre' approach is used:

- ☐ As part of an appraisal process
- ☐ As part of a process of training and development
- ☐ As part of a selection process
- ☐ As part of an exit interview process

13.2 In the context of 'best practice' employment protection law, in which of the following circumstances is dismissal of an employee automatically considered unfair?

- ☐ Selection for redundancy on the basis of age
- ☐ Misconduct
- ☐ Marriage to an employee of a key competitor
- ☐ Incompetence

13.3 Which of the following is associated with recruitment rather than selection?

- ☐ Assessment centres
- ☐ Interviews
- ☐ Advertising copy
- ☐ Psychometric testing

13.4 Which **FOUR** of the following are factors identified in Kirkpatrick's model for evaluating training events?

- ☐ Reaction
- ☐ Tutor knowledge
- ☐ Behaviour
- ☐ Cost
- ☐ Quality of materials
- ☐ Learning
- ☐ Results
- ☐ Number of interactions

13.5 David Kolb identified a four stage model representing

- ☐ A quality evaluation framework.
- ☐ A cycle of learning from experience.
- ☐ A career planning and development framework.
- ☐ A way of assessing the value of training events.

13.6 The set of activities designed to familiarise a new employee with an organisation is called:

- ☐ Job analysis
- ☐ Induction
- ☐ Selection
- ☐ Manipulation and co-optation

13.7 Recruitment involves:

- ☐ Advertising a vacancy and interviewing
- ☐ Conducting interviews and tests
- ☐ Advertising a vacancy and initial screening of candidates
- ☐ Ensuring that contract negotiation complies with organisational policy

13.8 Intelligence, aptitudes and disposition are often factors identified in:

- ☐ A job description
- ☐ Appraisal targets
- ☐ A person specification
- ☐ 360 degree documentation

13.9 The concept of 'reliability' of staff selection techniques means:

- ☐ Effective testing of a candidate's desire for the job and natural abilities
- ☐ Overcoming poor performance in the interview due to nervousness
- ☐ That if the test is repeated a consistent test score would be achieved
- ☐ Choosing the best candidate every time

13.10 In employment protection law, which of the following would constitute unfair dismissal?

- ☐ Dismissal because the employer has ceased to carry on the business
- ☐ Dismissal because the employer has relocated the place of work
- ☐ Dismissal because demand for the type of work done by the employee(s) is expected to decline
- ☐ Dismissal because the employee is pregnant

13.11 **Job rotation involves:**

☐ A redesign of a person's post based upon job analysis

☐ The movement of an individual to another post in order to gain experience

☐ The expansion and enrichment of a person's job content

☐ The relocation of a post holder in order to benefit from the experience of a number of potential mentors

13.12 **360 degree feedback is part of a system that encourages:**

☐ Organisational appraisal based on feedback from customers and suppliers

☐ Organisational appraisal based on relative industry and competitor performance

☐ Performance appraisal based on feedback from peers, subordinates, line managers and even external parties

☐ Personal appraisal based on line manager feedback and self-appraisal documentation

Answers to objective test questions

1 Organisational structures

1.1   The correct answer is: Strategic alliance.

Strategic alliances are simply agreements between parties. The company's plan is not a joint venture because no separate company is being formed. It is not licensing because the other party will not be manufacturing a product or using a brand name. It is not outsourcing because no activities are being relocated.

1.2   The correct answers are:

- Social arrangement
- Collective goals
- Controlled performance

Business organisations are social arrangements because they are run by and employ individuals. There are collective goals (organisational strategy) and controlled performance (monitoring of progress towards goals and corrective action taken if necessary).

Not all organisations have synergy or are specialised. Whilst the exchange of products or services is often a characteristic, it is not always the case (for example not-for-profit organisations that provide goods or services for nothing in return).

1.3   The correct answer is:

Profit-oriented organisation	Non-profit oriented organisation
Maximisation of wealth	Provision of goods/services

The objective of profit-making organisations is to generate wealth for the owners. Not-for-profit organisations have the objective of providing goods and services (such as health and education).

1.4

Term	Action
Horizontal integration	A company that makes toothbrushes decides to buy a toothpaste company.
Backwards vertical integration	Bixons Co, a retailer of electronic devices decides to buy NoxConn Co, which owns and runs a string of electronic device factories in the far east.
Shared service centre	A multinational is considering how it does IT support internally. The IT department in one of its locations is so good the company decides to shut down all its other IT departments. It will give greater funding to the single IT department, so it can help the whole company.
Forwards vertical integration	A company decides to buy the retail company it has traditionally sold its goods to.

Horizontal integration involves moving into products that are complementary or competitive.

Vertical integration involves moving into operations up or down the supply chain. Backwards means becoming a supplier and forwards means becoming a customer of your existing business.

Shared services centres consolidate processing operations in one location.

1.5   The correct answer is: Creating the maximum output for minimum input.

Efficient and effective business processes create the maximum output for the minimum input. Quality and value for money are not relevant to efficiency and effectiveness.

1.6 The correct answers are:

- We will encourage diversity in the workplace
- We intend to be the best airline in the world
- We aim to give excellent customer service

A mission statement sets out the organisation's basic purpose and what it is trying to achieve in general terms. The other options are goals because they are specific objectives.

1.7 The correct answers are:

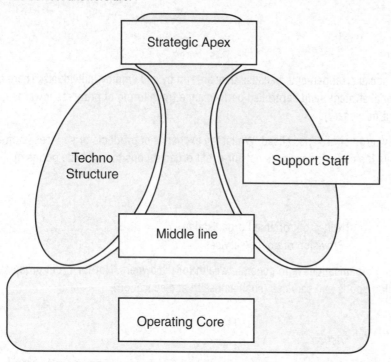

1.8 The correct answer is: Backwards vertical integration.

Horizontal integration involves moving into products that are complementary or competitive.

Vertical integration involves moving into operations up or down the supply chain. Backwards means becoming a supplier and forwards means becoming a customer of your existing business.

Business process outsourcing is a made-up term.

1.9 The correct answer is: The system and its components from its environment.

The system boundary is the outside edge of a system; therefore it does not relate to the boundaries within a system itself.

1.10 The correct answer is: Government funded.

Non-Governmental Organisations are independent, non-profit making organisations with social objectives.

1.11 The correct answer is: Primary objective.

A business is a profit-seeking organisation. The importance of profit may not be apparent from the organisation's vision and mission because these focus on the general purpose and direction of the organisation.

A primary objective of a business would be to generate or increase profits – so this would differentiate a business from a not-for-profit organisation. Secondary objectives are driven by primary objectives. They may not indicate a business because a not-for-profit organisation may have similar secondary objectives to a profit seeking one (eg reduce staff costs).

1.12 The correct answer is: Making profits.

Non-governmental organisations are defined by the World Bank as 'private organisations that pursue activities to relieve suffering, promote the interests of the poor, protect the environment, provide basic social services or undertake community development'. They are generally not profit-oriented.

1.13 The correct answer is: Geographical dispersion.

Geographical dispersion is a consideration for a more detailed discussion around how wide the organisation can/must be.

1.14 The correct answer is: Open.

An open system is connected to and interacts with its environment.

Closed systems are isolated from their environment. Entropy and decoupling are aspects of systems thinking but are not a type of systems thinking.

1.15 The correct answer is: Matrix.

In a matrix structure an employee may report to a line manager as well as a product or project manager. This encourages employee flexibility and multiple reporting.

1.16 The correct answer is: Outsource partners.

Mintzberg's organisation includes: the operating core, technostructure, middle line, strategic apex and support staff.

1.17 The correct answer is: Efficient use of resources.

Public sector organisations aim to use their resources efficiently. Profits and losses are not the main concerns of these organisations because they seek to provide public services. Charitable donations are not an objective of public sector organisations.

1.18 The correct answer is: Mutual organisations.

Mutuals are primarily in business to provide services to their customers. They are not owned by shareholders whom they have to pay a share of their profit to.

---

2 Corporate governance and regulation

2.1 The correct answer is: Increasing taxation.

Increasing taxation lowers demand in the economy because people have less of their own money after tax for consumption or saving/investment. Increasing public expenditure should increase the level of consumer demand. Decreasing taxation has the opposite effect. Lowering interest rates should stimulate investment (by companies) and consumer expenditure, even if only after a time lag.

2.2 The correct answer is: The chairman and chief executive are different individuals in order to prevent one person having too much power within the company.

It is good corporate governance to reduce the power any one individual has in a company and therefore it is important to separate the roles of chairman and chief executive. There is no reason why a chairman cannot hold other directorships providing this does not breach any other corporate governance rules.

2.3 The correct answer is:

Term	Action
Buffering	A housing charity offers to send a senior management team member to a government department to discuss the impact of proposed new squatting laws
Corporate political activity	Salco prides itself in being involved in the political process

Term	Action
Bridging	Erin, an employee of Ertbank, has a defined role in monitoring upcoming legislation that will affect the bank's operation

Buffering is active, and although the charity is sending a team member to discuss, the aim will be to influence. Erin's job is more passive, and is bridging. Corporate political activity describes both terms more broadly.

2.4 The correct answer is: Economic.

This is the responsibility to the shareholder and other directly linked parties to keep the costs of the company low.

Although you could argue that the company is just taking advantage of a grey area of the law, the fact that many countries alter laws to stop this kind of action shows that it is more comfortably part of the economic responsibility.

The ethical and philanthropic responsibilities are more about giving time or money to things that society wants. This would not cover tax avoidance.

2.5 The correct answer is: Treat this stakeholder as a key player when formulating future strategies.

The scenario suggests that the stakeholder has high power (ability to close down operations) and high influence (considerable influence is stated) and therefore, according to Mendelow, they should be treated as a key player.

2.6 The correct answer is: Employment protection.

The other areas are dealt with by a combination of best practice, codes and some legislation.

2.7 The correct answer is: Increased competition.

Increased competition exerts a downward pressure on prices as more companies compete for business by offering lower prices. Lower prices can only be sustained if businesses become more efficient and reduce their cost base.

Regulation may be used to curb excessive prices, but this may not improve efficiency. Public ownership reduces efficiency because there will be no competition in the market. Oligopoly means there will be a few businesses in the markets, but they may operate cartels which reduces competition and efficiency.

2.8 The correct answer is: The achievement of best practice.

Enlightened self-interest is the belief that long-term shareholder value can be generated from well-managed relationships with other stakeholders. Best practice helps with the achievement of well-managed relationships.

2.9 The correct answers are:

- Long-term projects may be prevented by managerial short-termism – the long-term interest of shareholders conflicts with the short-term objectives of managers.

- Owners of small businesses may lose control of the organisation when it grows and it is necessary to appoint managers to run the business – owners of the business lose control to management.

- The financial independence of an organisation may be reduced when additional shares or loans are required – the interest of existing shareholders is affected by giving rights to new shareholders or loan providers.

The other options only affect one set of stakeholders – the business's management – therefore there is no conflict.

2.10 The correct answers are:

- Shareholders
- Bankers

Return on investment will be of greatest importance to the shareholders and bankers – both of which have a financial interest in the company.

2.11 The correct answer is: Time available to devote to the role.

This is a major problem for non-executive directors, because they are likely to have other commitments. You should have had to think through the other options, however. Some of the advantages of non-executive directors are that they offer a comfort factor for third parties such as investors and suppliers; they have a wider perspective and (hopefully) no vested interest; and they have a combination of knowledge/expertise and detachment.

2.12 The correct answer is: An increase in public expenditure.

The other options would have the reverse effect because less money would be spent in the economy. Increasing public expenditure should increase the level of consumer demand and therefore the level of economic activity.

2.13 The correct answer is: An increasingly prominent role for non-executive directors.

Non-executive directors should provide a balancing influence and play a key role in reducing conflicts of interest between management and shareholders.

2.14 The correct answer is: Prevention of fraudulent claims by contractors.

Corporate governance focuses to a large extent on preventing directors from abusing their power. Prevention of fraudulent claims by contractors is not a major benefit of good corporate governance.

2.15 The correct answer is: Corporate governance.

Corporate governance is the system by which organisations are directed and controlled.

2.16 The correct answer is: The relationship between price and demand in a particular market.

Inflation, investment and unemployment are all macroeconomic factors. Price and demand within a particular market is a microeconomic factor.

2.17 The correct answer is: It should be independent of management actions.

Written codes of ethics set out values, not attitudes to risk. They should be independent of management actions. Non-compliance should not be supported and they are based on ethics not law.

2.18 The correct answer is: Philanthropic responsibilities

Philanthropic: these are desired rather than required of businesses. In Europe the application of this layer tends to be towards investing in communities and having responsible business practices, whereas in America it tends to focus on charitable donations.

3 The finance function

3.1 The correct answer is: Strategic management accounting.

Strategic management accounting involves considering a range of information from internal and external sources, including financial and non-financial information.

3.2 The correct answer is: Treasury.

The interest rate is the price of money. A rise in interest rates will raise the price of borrowing, and increase the interest that can be made on surplus funds.

3.3 The correct answer is: The financial transactions recording section.

The recording of financial transactions ensures that the business has an accurate record of its revenue, assets, liabilities and capital and this record allows the standard of stewardship to be monitored and reported on.

3.4 The correct answers are:

- Measurement of actual performance and comparison against targets
- Establishment of standards or targets to express planned performance
- Follow-up action to correct adverse results or to exploit favourable variances

Control systems set standards, measure performance and provide feedback to correct adverse results or exploit favourable balances. They do not devise plans, measure non quantifiable 'ideals' or identify deviations from the plan.

3.5 The correct answer is: External reporting.

Legal rules and accounting standards are used to prepare external reporting information.

3.6 The correct answer is: The Management Accountant.

The Management Accountant provides information for management: cost accounting, budgets and budgetary control and financial management of projects. The Financial Accountant is responsible for routine accounting, accounting reports, cashiers' duties and cash control. A Treasurer would be responsible for treasury management: raising and investing funds and cash flow control. The Finance Director approves the budget.

3.7 The correct answer is: Financial reporting.

The FRC and IASB accounting standards are involved in financial reporting.

3.8 The correct answers are:

- Providing shareholders with information
- Providing management with information
- Ensuring the availability of working capital
- Providing information to stakeholders

These are functions of the finance department. Quality control, production capacity and inventory management are the responsibility of operations. The sales revenue is the responsibility of sales.

3.9 The correct answers are:

- Arranging finance
- Administrating corporate tax affairs
- Management of foreign currency holdings

Variance analysis is associated with management accounting. Financial accounting ratios and asset revaluations are the responsibility of the financial accountants.

3.10 The correct answer is: Tailored response.

By centralising the finance function of a company to a single location efficiencies are improved. This may lead to reduction in headcount, and pooling of knowledge. However, the local finance team may have been able to understand local requirements better.

3.11 The correct answer is: Restricted access to loan finance.

Finance may be hard to come by because the financial health of the firm (ability to maintain and pay off loans) is understated. The other options are impacts of fraudulently overstating results.

3.12 The correct answer is: Identification of areas of potential risk.

One of the prerequisites for fraud is opportunity. Identifying areas of potential risk should reduce the opportunities to commit fraud.

3.13 The correct answer is: Internal reporting.

For internal reporting to be effective it is likely that some form of finance function would be needed in each centre so they are closer to what is happening.

3.14 The correct answers are:

- Guiding managers on how to achieve company objectives
- Allocating finite company resources
- Communicating a company's plans

It is not a purpose of budgets to support or help in the preparation of financial reporting information.

3.15 The correct answers are:

All variances should be investigated   **False**

Only material variances need to be investigated. How big the variance is will depend on the size of the organisation and how important it finds the subject of the variance

Variances are only possible after budgeting   **True**

Without a plan to measure progress against, variances become at best guess-work

Budgets help to identify the need for a loan   **True**

A cashflow budget or forecast is useful for identifying cash deficits

Budgets are made by the treasury function   **False**

Budgets are generally made by management accountants. Treasury has a focus on the funding of the company.

3.16 The correct answer is: (ii) and (iv)

Inventory reports can highlight wasteful cash invested in stock that is not needed.

There are few requirements over budgets. They are not required to be included in the financial statements and there is no stipulation over how often they are required to be produced. That is up to the business.

Allowing informed decision making is arguably the main aim of the entire finance function.

3.17 The correct answer is: $25,000.

$125,000 \times 0.2 = 25,000$

This means that borrowing will be a maximum of 20% of shareholders' funds.

3.18 The correct answer is: Add value.

The independent business partner model states that the role of the finance function is to add value not create value.

4 The technology and information function

4.1 The correct answer is: An extranet.

An extranet is in effect an intranet with the addition of permitted access to authorised external parties.

4.2 The correct answer is: Operational.

Systems at the operational level are used to process transactions and help operational managers track the organisation's day-to-day operational activities.

Strategic information tends to be high level and long term in nature. Tactical information is for medium term decision making by middle management. Executive is not a term recognised in the 'levels of information'.

4.3 The correct answer is: Web 2.0.

Web 2.0 applications include blogs and social networking sites.

B2C is the transactions which go on between businesses that sell to consumers (as opposed to businesses that sell direct to other businesses).

E-Commerce is the term that relates to trading activity that takes advantage of online/internet functionality.

Teleworking relates to employees that are able to work from a remote location (eg home) this is enabled by technology such as the internet.

4.4 The correct answer is: It has a single supply chain.

A virtual company is one that is made up of a number of smaller individual entities that work on projects together. They have the benefits of a larger organisation, such as economies of scale and low cost base, but they are also able to respond to changes to the environment quickly because they do not have a rigid structure.

The lack of rigid structure means there is often more than one supply chain – depending on which entity has capacity at any point in time.

4.5 The correct answer is: Cloud service.

This is an on demand service being driven by equipment run by a third party. This company is offering cloud computing. A WAN would be a wide network within an organisation. Similarly, grid computing, is when assets within the company are being used, although apart from that it describes this situation very well. The system is acting somewhat as an ES, as it is creating easy outputs, but the relationship is still best described by cloud computing.

4.6 The correct answer is: Data integrity and elimination of duplication.

Integrity and removal of duplication are always stated as key benefits of databases which are single data sources. They may be secure and not open to all (some may be protected). They are not involved in devolving responsibility – they just store data.

4.7 The correct answer is: Decision-based software.

Decision based software provides managers with the information and analysis tools to enable them to make decisions.

4.8 The correct answer is: Tactical.

Information at the tactical level within an organisation is designed to help middle managers monitor and control operations.

4.9 The correct answer is: Replacing inefficient parallel processes with efficient sequential processes.

If IT is to enhance business processes it is necessary to replace existing processes with new ones, otherwise the same old processes will continue. It cannot reduce delays in decision making because it is up to management when they take a decision.

Replacing separate inefficient parallel processes with efficient sequential ones means a single, more efficient process that is easier to control.

4.10 The correct answers are:

Architecture	Description
Mesh	All computers in the company can communicate directly with one another through a number of possible routes.
Bus	A central cable or spine exists, through which all computers in the company communicate.
Star	A central server is connected to all computers and helps them communicate.
Tree	A central server is connected to a number of other servers, and these servers each have a collection of computers attached to them.

Allocating mesh should have been ok, even if you didn't know what it meant. The image makes sense. Similarly, the star should work as an image. This leaves bus and tree. Tree has branching server relationships, this should have helped you get the right answer even if you didn't remember this niche part of the syllabus.

4.11　The correct answer is: E-commerce.

E-commerce (or online trading) opens up the global market for an organisation.

EDI provides more efficient transmission of data, teleworking provides a more efficient way of utilising/motivating staff. Penetration marketing aids in low cost penetration to a market.

4.12　The correct answer is: Developments in technology and information systems.

Virtual team working is made possible by developments in communications and other technology, enabling people to work together even when they are not physically located in the same place.

4.13　The correct answer is: CAD and CAM technologies.

The practical application of CAD and CAM technologies, rather than any general outlook or philosophy, are responsible for increased control over design and production using machinery.

4.14　The correct answer is: Customer relationship management (CRM).

Customer relationship management systems are software applications which specialise in providing information concerning an organisation's products, services and customers.

4.15　The correct answer is: An expert system.

Expert systems allow general users to benefit from knowledge and techniques of human experts.

4.16　The correct answer is: Customer relationship management system.

The key aspects of the statement is the management of relationships and customer information.

An expert system is a database that holds specialised knowledge and data and allows the user to input information for the system to interpret and provide a logical decision.

E-commerce is the term that relates to trading activity that takes advantage of online/internet functionality.

Cloud computing refers to the delivery of computing as a service rather than a product, whereby shared resources, software, and information are provided to computers over a network (typically the internet).

4.17　The correct answer is: Tactical.

Information at the tactical level within an organisation is designed to help middle managers monitor and control operations.

4.18　The correct answer is: Big Data analytics relies on digital information.

Information may be written, verbal or confidential, but if it is not digitised it cannot be analysed by Big Data analytics.

5 System implementation and business strategy

5.1　The correct answer is: Change as occurring through a series of restraining and driving forces.

Lewin's force field analysis is based on restraining and driving forces.

5.2　The correct answer is: Assembly and maintenance of a suitably skilled workforce

If the Information Systems function is outsourced, the organisation does not need to assemble and maintain a suitable IS workforce in-house.

5.3   The correct answer is: Negotiation and agreement.

Negotiation and agreement compensates those who lose out for example through the use of redundancy packages.

Whereas,

Facilitation and support is used where resistance is the result of insecurity and anxiety and training will be effective.

Manipulation and co-option is used to deal with the main individuals at the centre of the resistance by presenting partial and potentially misleading information.

Coercion is the method of last resort and involves the use or threat of force to see the change pushed through.

5.4   The correct answer is: An application control.

These are controls to ensure accurate, complete and valid data.

General controls are physical restrictions. Implicit controls are fictitious.

5.5   The correct answer is: To replace conventional documentation with structured electronically transmitted data.

One aim of Electronic Data Interchange (EDI) is to replace conventional documentation (eg invoices) with structured electronic data.

5.6   The correct answer is: Threat of new entrants.

The marketing tactic of making key accessories unique to a particular product discourages competitors from offering substitute products because the costs of so doing will be greater and entry into the market made more difficult. It does not alter the balance of power of suppliers or customers nor affect the intensity of competitive rivalry.

5.7   The correct answer is: Outsourcing.

Service level agreements (SLAs) are contractual agreements negotiated between an organisation and another organisation to which it is outsourcing an aspect of its operations. The purpose of the SLA is to specify the level of service that the external organisation is required to provide.

5.8   The correct answers are:

*   Less risky than direct
*   Problems are likely to be in one area

Phased/modular changeover is less risky than a single direct changeover and any problems should be in one area. Whereas, direct changeover minimises workload and cost and parallel running provides a way of verifying results of the new system.

5.9   The correct answer is: Service bureaux.

Timeshare is charged on a time-used basis and facilities management is traditionally premises-related services. Multiple sourcing involves outsourcing different areas of the IS function to a range of suppliers.

5.10   The correct answer is: A cookie.

Cookies are used to store information about website visitors.

5.11   The correct answer is: Refreezing.

The final stage in Lewin's three stage model of change is called refreezing and describes the process of fixing a certain behaviour into individuals or groups.

5.12   The correct answer is: Passive resistance.

Active resignation is a made up term. The other options are other possible responses to change that don't involve regressive or non-learning behaviour.

5.13 The correct answer is: 2 and 4.

Outsourcing functions like IT simplifies the structure of an organisation and reduces ongoing operational costs, but because support is external to the organisation, there may be a greater lead time required for resolving IT issues. Because there is less direct control over subcontractor's employees, long term projects, in particular, may be prone to disruption.

5.14 The correct answer is: The value chains of suppliers, channels and the customer.

Porter defined a value chain within an organisation as the primary activities and support activities within the organisation. He also argued that the value chains of individual organisations are linked in a value system of suppliers, distributors and customers. The value chain of each organisation is a part of the total value system.

5.15 The correct answer is: An outsourced IS function.

Where an organisation outsources its IS function, it becomes the client and the outsourcing partner becomes the vendor.

5.16 The correct answer is:

Encourages new entrants	Erects a barrier to new entrants
Low competition	High capital costs

Low levels of competition in an industry make it more attractive for new entrants. High capital costs involve risk and fund raising challenges which can act as a barrier to new entrants.

5.17 The correct answer is: Remedy software defects.

Corrective maintenance is carried out to correct residual faults. The other options are enhancements (perfective maintenance) or take account of anticipated changes in the processing environment (adaptive maintenance).

5.18 The correct answer is: Structured data and standard business documents.

Electronic data interchange can be used to link an organisation to its supplier (or suppliers) through a purchase/sales order system. The ability of their different information systems to exchange data requires the use of structured data and standard business documents.

6 Operations management and the organisation

6.1 The correct answer is: Recognising the supply chain and linkages in a value system.

Supply chain partnerships develop when customers and suppliers recognise the supply chain and linkages in a value system.

6.2 The correct answers are:

- Inbound logistics
- Marketing and sales
- Service

The other primary activities are operations and outbound logistics.

6.3 The correct answer is: Suppliers, manufacturers, distribution channels and customers' value chains.

Porter's value system reflects the importance of adding value at all stages in the supply chain – from the first supplier in the chain to the end-user or customer.

6.4 The correct answer is: Purchasing and supply.

Reck and Long's strategic positioning tool identified a four-phase development of purchasing within organisations.

6.5 The correct answers are:

Term	Process part
Transforming inputs	The trained accountant
Transformed inputs	The client's transactional data
Outputs	The financial statements
Transformation process	The audit

The accountant transforms the transactional data by the audit process into the output (financial statements).

6.6 The correct answer is: A primary activity that refers to receipt, storage and inward distribution of raw materials.

According to Porter's Value Chain, inbound logistics is a primary activity that refers to receipt, storage and inward distribution of raw materials.

6.7 The correct answer is: 1, 2, 3 and 4.

Recycling reduces the amount of waste the business produces. Energy efficiency reduces the amount of energy it needs and therefore the amount of pollution caused. Careful selection of suppliers (for example those that are environmentally friendly) helps reduce its impact as well. Buying raw materials locally means that less pollution is used in transporting the goods.

6.8 The correct answer is: Single, multiple, delegated and parallel.

Sourcing strategies can be to use single, multiple, delegated or parallel suppliers.

6.9 The correct answer is: Products are developed in response to market signals.

In a demand network, products are 'pulled' into existence in response to demand signals.

6.10 The correct answer is: Velocity

Velocity relates to the 3 V's used to define 'Big Data'.

The missing element of the analysis in the list above is variation in demand.

6.11 The correct answer is: Strategic.

Reck and Long developed the strategic positioning tool.

6.12 The correct answer is: Sheila.

Steve is in firm infrastructure.

Sunny is in procurement.

Sam is in technology development.

These are all support activities.

Sheila is in after sales service – a primary activity.

6.13 The correct answer is: Government regulation of the industry.

The other forces are bargaining power of suppliers and rivalry amongst current competitors in the industry.

6.14 The correct answer is: A number of different companies.

A supply chain is an interconnecting group of organisations which relate to each other through linkages between different processes and activities involved in producing products/services to the ultimate consumer.

6.15 The correct answer is: Comparison of a service, practice or process against one or more similar activities.

Although the other options involve some form of comparison, they do not imply comparison against similar activities.

6.16   The correct answers are:

Phase	Characteristic
Passive	Purchasing reacts to requests from other departments
Independent	Recognition that negotiation with suppliers is important
Supportive	Emphasis on co-ordination and compliance with centrally negotiated contracts
Integrative	Suppliers are viewed as partners

Each characteristic is an element directly found in the relevant phase of Reck and Long's model.

6.17   The correct answer is:

In operations management **resources** are used to **create** outputs that **fulfil** specific **market requirements**.

This is the process of operations management.

7 Quality Management

7.1   The correct answer is: Examples of internal failure costs.

Corrective work, the cost of scrap and materials lost are examples of internal failure costs.

7.2   The correct answer is: Quality circles.

Quality circles were advocated initially by the Japanese management theorist Ishikawa. Quality circles are meetings of invited employees from different sections of an organisation, to discuss quality issues and hopefully agree on ideas for improvements. Empowerment is another aspect of employee participation and involvement, but is concerned with giving decision-making powers to employees.

7.3   The correct answer is: Registration under the standards required for quality certification.

Quality certification requires approval of such materials.

7.4   The correct answer is: Balanced scorecards.

The balanced scorecard approach to quality measurement focuses on customer, operational and financial perspectives.

7.5   The correct answer is: A prevention of quality failures through equipment faults.

Productive maintenance is an approach that is intended to ensure that every machine in a production process performs its required tasks so that its output is not disrupted. The approach seeks to eliminate as much non-productive time on machines as possible.

7.6   The correct answer is: A framework for bringing about quality improvement to a process or system.

Plan-Do-Check-Act (PDCA) was developed by Deming as an approach for improving the quality of a process or system.

7.7   The correct answer is: Internal failure cost.

Internal failure costs include the cost of materials or components lost or scrapped in the production process, re-working costs, and losses from selling faulty output at reduced prices. The other categories of quality costs are appraisal costs (or inspection costs), prevention costs and external failure costs. Inspection costs are the costs of checking finished goods. Prevention costs are costs incurred prior to making a product or delivering a service, to prevent substandard production. External failure costs are costs arising from inadequate quality, where the problem is identified after the finished product or service has been delivered to the customer.

7.8   The correct answer is: Effective processes for documentation and control.

To gain ISO accreditation an organisation is required to submit documentation to show that their processes meet ISO requirements. The other options are not necessarily required.

7.9 The correct answer is: To meet customer expectations.

A key focus of quality under the Japanese approach is customer satisfaction, which relies on meeting customer needs and expectations.

7.10 The correct answer is: Customers.

Servqual involves comparing aspects of the service that customers receive with their expectations of what they should receive. To do this, there must be feedback from customers.

7.11 The correct answer is: The application of Japanese managerial practices into Western culture.

This theory was produced by Ouchi in 1981.

7.12 The correct answer is: Operations management practices of structurise, systematise, sanitise, standardise and self-discipline.

The 5-S model describes operations management practices of structurise, systemise, sanitise and self-discipline. It does not describe internal analysis or a form of six sigma.

7.13 The correct answer is: Effective processes for documentation and control.

To gain ISO accreditation an organisation is required to submit documentation to show that their processes meet ISO requirements. The other options are not necessarily required.

7.14 The correct answer is: Production oriented.

A manufacturer with a production orientation concentrates upon production efficiencies and cost cutting because it believes that this will be enough to sell the product in whatever quantities can be manufactured.

7.15 The correct answer is: 180 degree feedback.

180 degree feedback is a form of feedback on personal performance.

7.16 The correct answer is: Integrity.

Integrity is a hygiene factor.

8 Managing capacity and inventory

8.1 The correct answer is: An inventory management method that concentrates effort on the most important items.

ABC is an inventory management method that concentrates effort on the most important items.

8.2 The correct answer is: Fixed.

In a fixed layout the product being created remains in a fixed location and people, materials and other resources travel to it.

8.3 The correct answer is: The risk of delay in production against the cost of holding inventory of Ubbo.

When deciding the quantity of an item to be ordered, the major factors to be balanced are whether to order more, and incur inventory holding costs, or to order less, and risk delaying production because there is too little material.

8.4 The correct answer is: ABC.

ABC inventory management focuses on the most expensive items as a priority as their value justifies the extra administrative effort.

8.5 The correct answer is: Computer numerical control.

Although the difference between this and robots is ambiguous, robots are more associated with manipulating components or checking them, rather than creation. CNC usually describes cutting or working raw materials in some way.

The other two systems are not related to manufacture directly.

8.6   The correct answer is: Just-in-time.

Producing or purchasing items as they are needed is referred to as Just-in-Time (JIT).

8.7   The correct answer is: Inventory system based on economic order quantities.

EOQ stands for Economic Order Quantity.

8.8   The correct answer is: Cell.

Process is departmental, with the product moving around to specialised teams. Product is a tailored approach where the flow changes depending on the product. Fixed has specialist teams travel to the product, as it is hard to move. Cell is where a team is able to do everything needed to turn raw materials into a finished product.

8.9   The correct answer is: A high variety of tasks are performed in one place.

In a fixed position production layout, the product being created stays in one place and plant and staff move to it. Therefore a high variety of tasks are performed in one place.

8.10   The correct answers are:

- Customer relationship management system
- Big Data

These are mainly used to understand the company's customers and environment better. The others are used to improve rate of flow and efficiency of a process.

8.11   The correct answer is: Focuses inventory management on the 20% of items (representing 80% of inventory expenditure) which need careful monitoring.

The other options refer to continuous inventory systems or periodic inventory (or bin) systems.

8.12   The correct answer is: Activity is adjusted depending upon demand.

Under a chase demand capacity plan, the activity level responds to changes in demand.

8.13   The correct answer is: Reduce production bottlenecks.

Optimised Production Technologies focus on the removal of production bottlenecks.

9 The marketing concept

9.1   The correct answer is: Because customers that share certain characteristics are likely to exhibit similar buying behaviour.

The aim of segmentation is to allow marketing efforts to be identified and targeted more effectively by grouping customers by identifiable characteristics relevant to buying behaviour.

9.2   The correct answer is: An entire market with a single marketing mix.

Undifferentiated marketing involves producing a single product and getting as many customers as possible to buy it. There is no market segmentation.

9.3   The correct answer is: Undifferentiated.

An undifferentiated policy involves producing a single product and hoping to get as many customers as possible to buy it – segmentation is ignored entirely.

9.4   The correct answer is: Demographic.

Demographic information is freely available and relatively cheap to obtain. For example much of it is provided by the Government. The other options require either further analysis of existing data or new research on behalf of the organisation. These options are therefore more expensive.

9.5   The correct answer is: Strategic marketing.

Strategic marketing involves identifying the products and markets the organisation wishes to operate in. Mass marketing involves marketing to an entire market. Target marketing is focussing marketing effort on a particular target. Tactical marketing focuses on the short-term and the marketing mix.

9.6   The correct answer is: Product orientated.

Product orientated organisations focus on product features.

9.7   The correct answer is: Target a single market segment with a specific product.

Whole market/single product is undifferentiated positioning, a distinct marketing mix per segment is differentiated targeting. The other option is incorrect because it refers to a range of products.

9.8   The correct answer is: Product orientated.

A product oriented organisation focuses on product development and features.

9.9   The correct answer is: It is concerned with the satisfaction of customer needs over the long term.

Marketing is concerned with meeting customer needs of the long term. Sales, or selling, is concerned with immediate issues of selling the product in the short term.

9.10   The correct answer is: Transferring finished goods to intermediaries who then have the task of selling those goods to consumers.

'Push' refers to the transfer of goods to third parties – the term is used because the manufacturer 'pushes' goods onto wholesalers or similar intermediaries.

9.11   The correct answer is: Education.

Family lifecycle stage, gender and age are examples of demographic bases for market segmentation. Education is a segmentation base on its own.

9.12   The correct answer is: A focus on customer needs.

A marketing orientation involves structuring an organisation's activities around the needs of the customer.

9.13   The correct answer is: (i), (ii), (iii), (iv) and (v).

Ethical issues arise in all business areas such as materials used (pollution), quality of goods (safety), advertising (targeting vulnerable people), wages (low-pay in developing countries) and packaging (recyclable).

9.14   The correct answer is: Lean orientation.

Organisations may be marketing oriented, sales oriented, product oriented or production oriented. Lean orientation is a made up term.

9.15   The correct answer is: 'Place', one component of the marketing mix.

Distribution channels, transport, warehouse and sales outlets are examples of the 'place' component in the marketing mix. Promotion usually describe advertising and physical evidence usually describes the product's environment in a service industry. The other option is irrelevant because it refers to a service organisation – the locations in the question relate to traditional consumer goods.

9.16   The correct answer is: Customers and communication.

Effective product promotion is centred on customers and communication. The other options focus on the internal business rather than the consumers.

10 Marketing techniques

10.1 The correct answer is: Penetration pricing.

Penetration pricing is used to establish or increase market share. Skim pricing involves setting an initially high price for a product. Cost-plus involves adding a mark-up on cost. Market leader pricing involves following the price set by the dominant player in the market.

10.2 The correct answer is: Introduction, growth, maturity, decline.

The correct stages and sequence of the product life cycle are introduction, growth, maturity and decline.

10.3 The correct answer is: Promotion.

Promotion includes all marketing communications which let the public know about an organisation's products and services.

10.4 The correct answer is: Harvest.

The product has high market share in a market with low growth and is therefore a cash cow. A harvest strategy is most appropriate because growth is weakening. If growth was still strong then a hold strategy would have been appropriate.

Divest strategy would apply to products classed as 'Dog'.

Build strategy would be appropriate to products classed as 'Question Mark'.

10.5 The correct answer is: Zero level distribution.

Hessehoff's traditional distribution is one level, through a retailer. Selling direct to the consumer is zero level. Although the tour may be tailored to the customer, it isn't described well by interactive marketing. Marketing would need to be more shocking to be guerrilla in nature. BPR is a radical redesign of processes, and is usually more associated with the operations side of the business.

10.6 The correct answer is: Loss leader pricing.

Loss leaders are products that have a very low price set with the objective of attracting consumers to buy other products in the range with higher profit margins.

10.7 The correct answer is: Sales volume and time.

A product life cycle chart plots sales volume against time.

10.8 The correct answer is: Positioning.

The 7Ps in the extended marketing mix are Product, Price, Place, Promotion, People, Processes and Physical evidence.

10.9 The correct answer is: Personal and interactive.

Post-modern marketing seeks to get people involved with a tailored message that often invites sharing or action from the target. Although it is experiential, this is not part of the promotional mix categories.

10.10 The correct answer is: Customer Relationship Management (CRM).

The collecting and interpreting of a potentially large amount of data from multiple sources to customise the offering to customers is the primary concern of a CRM. A TPS may be a way of collecting that data, as may be an ES, but it would be the CRM that collated and presented the data in a way that would make tailoring possible. Digital-marketing through a website may involve using the results of Big Data and a CRM. It may also collect data if it allows customer interaction, but again a CRM is more clearly involved in Big Data.

10.11 The correct answer is: Viral marketing.

Viral marketing involves the use of pre-existing social networks to spread brand awareness or other marketing objectives.

10.12 The correct answer is: Quick and easy ability to provide pop-up advertising on-screen.

Pop-up adverts are regarded by most users as unhelpful and irritating and so not good when trying to achieve positive brand awareness.

The other options are often regarded as helpful or welcome by users.

10.13 The correct answer is: Experiential.

Primarily, Jane is attempting to create an emotional link between the target and her company.

Relationship is more interactive in nature, as is post-modern.

Although you could argue that Jane's campaign is shocking, and so Guerrilla, this is usually more imaginative. The aim is to create a buzz, something that will be talked about and so carry the company's message.

10.14 The correct answer is: Big Data marketing.

The definition of Big Data is very wide. In this case, trawling the web to use unconventional, high volume sources of data to understand customers is the clue.

If Ralph Moren was simply looking at the gender of people logging onto its own website, this would be closer to the use of a conventional CRM.

If Ralph Moren was trying to get a dialogue going with the customer, this would fit into relationship marketing.

The use of a web-page is e-marketing.

If Ralph Moren was using a message that changed depending on the inputs of the consumer, such as a game, this would fit post-modern marketing.

10.15 The correct answer is: Market growth and market maturity.

A shakeout would occur between market growth and market maturity (shaking some of the weaker 'players' out of the market).

10.16 The correct answer is:

Concept	Situation
An expert system	A website is able to take user inputs about their preferred climate and activities to suggest a perfect holiday.
Post-modern marketing	When a user points their camera-phone at another person, an app shows how a piece of clothing would look on them. Users are encouraged to upload pictures of themselves wearing the virtual clothing, to be used in the company website.
Big Data	A site is able to read your email, and analyse the photos you attach to your email. It uses this to tailor the adverts it shows you.
Relationship marketing	A company prides itself on never sending an email to a user without a prompt. Prompts include asking about recent purchases, and how they could improve the service, and making the user aware of a sale on an item they've indicated is a 'favourite'.

Concept	Situation	Explanation
An expert system	A website is able to take user inputs about their preferred climate and activities to suggest a perfect holiday.	An expert system takes complex user inputs and creates decisions without the need for expert human labour
Post-modern marketing	When a user points their camera-phone at another person, an app shows how a piece of clothing would look on them. Users are encouraged to upload pictures of themselves wearing the virtual clothing, to be used in the company website.	Post-modern marketing is characterised as: • Not static like a magazine advert • Tailored to the user • Interactive and immersive • Involves the customer in the brand
Big Data	A site is able to read your email, and analyse the photos you attach to your email. It uses this to tailor the adverts it shows you.	Big Data takes vast volumes of information from unstructured sources. Emails and pictures are not intended to be communication of preference to the company. Big Data makes them ways of tailoring the offering.
Relationship marketing	A company prides itself on never sending an email to a user without a prompt. Prompts include asking about recent purchases, and how they could improve the service, and making the user aware of a sale on an item they've indicated is a 'favourite'.	Relationship marketing sees the process as two way, and tries to avoid unsolicited communication.

10.17 The correct answer is: Setting an initially high price for a new product.

Market skimming involves setting an initially high price for a new product to take advantage of those willing to pay it.

11 Developments in marketing

11.1 The correct answer is: Demerit goods.

Demerit goods are goods considered to be unhealthy or damaging to society.

11.2 The correct answer is: 1. False 2. True.

A demerit good, although discouraged by society may still be legal. A merit good is seen as something to be encouraged, and is generally provided free of charge by the government.

11.3 The correct answers are:

•   Product
•   Price

To convince resistant employees that the marketing plan is a good idea, the plan itself may need to be changed (product) or the impact to employees, such as resources or pay (price). Place and promotion are unlikely to be affected, and may have already happened by this point.

11.4 The correct answer is: Place.

In the context of the internal marketing mix, place is how you deliver the message to your employees.

11.5   The correct answer is:

Category	Activity
Individualise	Badpigsco's website links with a popular social media website to integrate its data with candidate's previous jobs and narrow the search for a suitable job
Initiate	Candidates are encouraged to write a blog on the company website about their work placement. A voucher is given to the best entry every month
Involve	Badpigsco publishes an article monthly and invites candidates to discuss the issues raised
Integrate	The website has individualised settings that allow a candidate to set the frequency of communications received so as not to become a nuisance

11.6   The correct answers are:

- Individualise
- Initiate

Yolocorp is attempting to only engage with users who have an active interest in their film. They are also inviting user created content to be posted.

Individualise – activities should take a customer's interests and preferences into account

Involve – engaging conversations should be used to involve the customer in the interaction

Integrate – activities should be integrated into a customer's life so they do not become a nuisance

Initiate – customer-generated content should be encouraged

11.7   The correct answer is: A small business.

Social media may be useful to all types of organisation for a wide range of purposes. However, the use of existing infrastructure and reliance on users to spread a message can make it very cost-effective for small businesses that may not be able to afford other media.

11.8   The correct answer is: Unethical and legal.

The product is not breaking any laws. However, it would be seen as encouraging violent behaviour in children.

Ethical and legal (eg printing on recycled paper)

Unethical and legal (eg targeting young adults in an 'alcopops' advertising campaign)

Ethical but illegal (eg publishing stolen but revealing documents about mis-selling)

Unethical and illegal (eg passing off cheap imitation goods as designer brands)

11.9   The correct answer is: Employer branding.

This is a reason to engage in internal marketing. It makes, for example, attracting the right candidate for the job easier by creating a coherent brand amongst the workforce. The reasons the others are reasons for internal marketing being more difficult are below:

Flatter management structures, meaning that managers have more people reporting to them (a wider 'span of control').

A trend towards tele-working and 'virtual' organisation, so that staff may be geographically remote from the office, manager and each other.

Globalisation, creating increasingly diverse workforces and culturally distinctive units within the organisation, which pose barriers to 'mass' communication.

11.10 The correct answer is:

Category	Concern
Place	Frank had to find out about the trip from his friend, not reading the magazine where they advertised. The magazine is the place.
Price	Frank questions the flight carrier that the charity has chosen to transport the group to the country, arguing that they could travel just as well by freight ferry. Price is the cost of transport.
Process	Frank hasn't found it easy to put his information into the charity's website. It keeps rejecting his passport number as he isn't a UK national. The website is the process.
Product	Frank doesn't believe that building an orphanage is as important as helping in a local hospital. The orphanage is what the charity does – its product.

11.11 The correct answers are:

Type of marketing	Activity
Relationship	NiffNaff is a mobile phone network that prides itself on taking suggestions from its customers seriously
Viral	Aggracorp has filmed its factory staff singing and dancing in the hope this will be spread on social media
Guerrilla	Partyco organised an impromptu and possibly illegal party on government premises saying it could liven up any location. Press covered it eagerly and the message was spread exponentially
Post-modern	Winga, a brewer, used the location of customers from their phones to send interesting facts about the neighbourhood. It suggested bars where the customer could order their drinks. Customers would 'collect' these locations for prizes

NiffNaff is listening to its customers, and takes chances to build up a relationship.

Aggracorp hopes for exponential indirect marketing via social media.

Although the effect of this may be a viral campaign, the original event is a shocking one. This is guerrilla marketing.

Post modern relies on customised interactions with the customer to market through multiple media.

11.12 The correct answer is: Relationship marketing.

The maximisation of customer retention and satisfaction through two-way communication is known as relationship marketing.

Postmodern marketing is about giving the customer an experience that is customised to them. Experiential marketing involves providing the customer with an experience that creates an emotional connection between the person and the brand. E-marketing is a general term relating to all electronic marketing activities.

11.13 The correct answer is: Accepting orders online is only the first step – the challenge then is to deliver the product or service ordered.

For this to occur, efficient back-office procedures are vital.

12 Human resources management

12.1 The correct answer is: A hierarchy of needs.

Maslow's theory of motivation describes a hierarchy of needs from physical needs up to self-actualisation.

12.2 The correct answer is: The closure of another workplace within the vicinity that employs staff with similar skills.

This option clearly links the availability of workers to a set location. The other options affect supply nationally or within an industry.

12.3 The correct answers are:

- Overtime
- Reducing labour turnover, by reviewing possible causes

These would allow staff to work longer hours or motivate them to stay on. The company wants to reduce the workforce in this situation.

12.4 The correct answers are:

- Integrity
- Professional competence and due care

Darlene is considering misleading the client and work beyond her competence.

12.5 The correct answer is: If targets are not met then employees may become demotivated.

The main risk of performance related pay is demotivation. The other problems can either be overcome or are simply not relevant to PRP.

12.6 The correct answer is: The needs of individuals.

Content theories of motivation (eg Maslow, Hertzberg) focus on the needs of the individual.

12.7 The correct answer is: Force = Valence × Expectation.

Force = Valence × Expectation represents Victor Vroom's model of motivation.

12.8 The correct answer is: Scientific.

F W Taylor is associated with the scientific school of management thinking. These management theorists held the view that work problems can be resolved scientifically through experimentation and the analysis of the results, until an optimum solution is found.

12.9 The correct answer is: Adjustments to an individual's job content and role.

Job enlargement, enrichment and rotation are all methods of improving employee motivation by introducing changes to an individual's role.

12.10 The correct answer is: Significant influence by uncontrollable factors.

This tends to break the link between performance and reward.

12.11 The correct answer is: A valence.

According to Victor Vroom, valence is the strength of a person's preference for a certain outcome.

12.12 The correct answer is: The psychological contract.

The set of expectations between an organisation and its employees is known as a psychological contract.

12.13 The correct answer is: The mutual expectations of an employee and employer.

This is the psychological contract.

12.14 The correct answer is: It requires close monitoring of relationships and performance and therefore has a cost.

There is a cost implication of performance related pay against other methods of remuneration. However it links performance and reward and therefore encourages employees to act in a manner that benefits the organisation. Although not all employees receive the same pay rise, they all have the same opportunity to gain it.

12.15 The correct answer is: Process outcomes.

An HRM strategy should impact upon financial outcomes (cost of wages etc), behavioural outcomes (staff discipline etc) and performance outcomes (efficiency and effectiveness of employees). Processes are decided by those involved in managing the operation – such as the production director.

12.16 The correct answer is: Employees are considered as a resource to be controlled.

Under the human resource management approach, employees are viewed as assets or resources.

13 Human resources practices

13.1 The correct answer is: As part of a selection process.

An 'assessment centre' approach is used in the selection process.

13.2 The correct answer is: Selection for redundancy on the basis of age.

This constitutes unfair selection for redundancy (on the basis of age discrimination legislation): redundancy is potentially fair grounds for dismissal as long as the basis of selection is fair.

The other options are potentially fair grounds: there should be a reasonable attempt at performance or disciplinary management (warnings, training etc). Marriage to an employee of a key competitor is an example of 'substantial reasons' that would be considered by a tribunal.

13.3 The correct answer is: Advertising copy.

Assessment centres, interviews and psychometric testing are used in the selection process.

Advertising copy is part of advertising a vacancy and is therefore part of the recruitment process.

13.4 The correct answers are:

- Reaction
- Behaviour
- Learning
- Results

These are the factors identified by Kirkpatrick.

13.5 The correct answer is: A cycle of learning from experience.

Kolb suggested a four-stage learning cycle. Concrete experience, reflection, theorising and active experimentation.

13.6 The correct answer is: Induction.

The process where new employees are familiarised with an organisation is called their induction.

13.7 The correct answer is: Advertising a vacancy and initial screening of candidates.

Recruitment describes the process attracting suitable candidates to apply for selection. Interviews and tests are part of selection.

13.8 The correct answer is: A person specification.

These qualities focus on the person. A job description explains what is required in a job. The other options are part of an appraisal system.

13.9 The correct answer is: That if the test is repeated a consistent test score would be achieved.

In the context of selection techniques, reliability means the achievement of consistent results.

13.10 The correct answer is: Dismissal because the employee is pregnant.

The other options are circumstances defined as redundancy. Dismissal on the grounds of pregnancy is automatically considered to be unfair dismissal.

13.11 The correct answer is: The movement of an individual to another post in order to gain experience.

Job rotation involves individuals moving from post to post.

13.12 The correct answer is: Performance appraisal based on feedback from peers, subordinates, line managers and even external parties.

360 degree feedback includes appraisal 'from all angles'; subordinates, peers, line manager and possibly external parties.

Practice mock questions

Questions

1   Which of the following is a major factor affecting the demand for skilled labour in a particular region?

Select the most relevant option.

☐   The availability of government funding for training schemes

☐   The opening or closure of workplaces competing for the same skills

☐   A change in industry regulations regarding factory shift patterns

☐   The availability of skilled workers in that region

2   Which FOUR of the following affect the complexity and scope of an organisation's accounting systems?

☐   The industry within which the organisation operates

☐   The degree of decentralisation

☐   Manager performance and motivation

☐   Requirements to provide information to external parties

☐   The type of organisation

☐   The size of the organisation

☐   The organisational structure

3   Which TWO of the following are examples of indirect marketing?

☐   Writing an article for a trade journal

☐   Targeting individual customers with promotional material

☐   Posting 'blogs' online to draw attention to the organisation

☐   Providing free e-books on social media sites

4   Which of the following features is normally associated with Gartner's 3Vs definition of 'Big Data'?

Select the most relevant option.

☐   Value added

☐   Variation in demand

☐   Velocity

☐   Visibility

5   Which of the following is a potential advantage of the networked enterprise?

Select the most relevant option.

☐   Improved communication with customers and suppliers

☐   The value of commercial software increases as more people become involved

☐   Access to up to date processes

☐   More competition among suppliers may lower product process

6 **Which of the following is an advantage of a functional structure?**

Select the most relevant option.

☐ Horizontal coordination is easy

☐ Hierarchy overload will not occur

☐ Good levels of communication between different functions

☐ Expertise is pooled

☐ Innovation is encouraged

☐ Focuses on internal processes and inputs

---

7 **Which TWO of the following are considered to be 'liquidity' ratios?**

☐ Earnings per share

☐ Price/earnings ratio

☐ Dividend yield

☐ Current ratio

☐ Stock turn

☐ Profit per employee

☐ Return on sales

☐ Acid test

---

8 **Which FOUR of the following are NOT parts of the marketing dimensions?**

☐ Product

☐ Promotion

☐ Culture

☐ Price

☐ Strategy

☐ Production

☐ Tactics

---

9 **Which of the following is an essential feature of a written code of ethics?**

Select the most relevant option.

☐ It states the company values

☐ It is publically available

☐ It rewards non-compliance

☐ It is legally enforceable

10   **Which of the following marketing decisions is unlikely to raise ethical issues?**

Select the most relevant option.

☐   Working with competitors to ensure the market remains profitable

☐   Printing on recycled paper

☐   Targeting young adults in an 'alcopops' advertising campaign

☐   Highlighting onerous contract clauses included in the small print

☐   Passing off cheap imitation goods as designer brands

11   **Which of the following is NOT an intended feature of a virtual company model?**

Select the most relevant option.

☐   Improved flexibility and speed of operation

☐   The suppliers and resources are also available to rival operations

☐   Low investment in assets and hence less risk involved

☐   Injection of market forces into all the linkages in the value chain

12   **Which of the following normally represents the biggest challenge in reaping the benefits of centralised business support services, such as finance and IT?**

Select the most relevant option.

☐   Reducing headcount

☐   Setting up an effective shared service level agreement

☐   Achieving reduced premises and other overhead costs

☐   Knowledge sharing to improve quality of the service provided

☐   Consistent management of business data

13   Stakeholders are mostly interested in the success of the business, and this creates a common goal. However, in certain circumstances stakeholder interests may create conflicts with other stakeholder groups.

Which THREE of the following are examples of stakeholder interests being aligned?

☐   Shareholders demanding rising profits and customers wanting higher quality products

☐   The company operates a share save scheme where employees become shareholders in the company

☐   Employee demand for pay rises against the need for management to maximise profit

☐   Suppliers work in collaboration with the business on new product design to meet customer demands for product improvement

☐   The community wanting minimal environmental impact from the organisation but shareholders want the least costly option for disposing of waste chosen

☐   Directors may recommend that the business is taken over by another but shareholders want to remain independent

☐   Directors introduce a corporate social responsibility charter which increases its involvement in the local community

14   One of the ways in which marketing benefits society is by informing and educating consumers.

Which ONE of the following is NOT a benefit of marketing to society?

☐   It promotes and delivers desired products and services

☐   It provides practical information to assist customers in making a purchase

☐   It helps set and manage consumer expectations

☐   It provides the ability to more quickly upgrade products with advanced technology and quality features

☐   It provides a place for behavioural research

15   **CIMA's Ethical Guidelines make it clear that individuals must do which THREE of the following?**

☐   Observe the highest standards of conduct and integrity

☐   Ensure consistency is upheld in operating practices

☐   Base decision making on the primary stakeholder effected by the decision

☐   Uphold the good standing and reputation of the profession

☐   Refrain from any conduct which might discredit the profession

16   **A control system which forecasts differences between actual and planned outcomes and implements actions after the event to avoid such differences is known as:**

Select the most relevant option.

☐   Feedback

☐   Feedforward

☐   Open loop

☐   Activity based control

17   Though mostly discussed in relation to quoted companies, governance is an issue for all organisations.

Which FOUR of the following have been highlighted as risks or problems that can arise in organisations' systems of governance?

☐   Dominance by a single senior executive

☐   Irregular board meetings

☐   Audit committee comprised entirely of non-executive directors

☐   Lack of employee supervision

☐   Segregation of key roles

☐   Director bonus schemes based on company performance such as profitability

18   **Which THREE of the following tasks are NOT normally related with the internal audit function?**

☐   Reviewing internal controls, risk management systems and financial reports

☐   Financial ratio analysis

☐   Effective taxation administration

☐   Managing the data used by management to identify risks

☐   Identifying methods for prioritising and managing risks

☐   Reporting on how effective risk management controls are

☐   Reporting on variances between the expected and actual financial results

☐   Prevention and detection of fraud and intentional misstatements in financial statements

---

19   **Which THREE of the following are NOT characteristics of a well-arranged strategic alliance?**

☐   Differing management styles and operational models used

☐   Organisations are stronger by working together

☐   The strengths and weaknesses of one party should complement those of the other

☐   One of the parties should gain a market leadership position

☐   The risks of the venture are shared

☐   Marketing and other advice and support is provided

☐   Acting in a certain geographical location as a distribution channel

---

20   Information technology may be the driving force of organisational change.

Which FOUR of the following are benefits of an organisation having an IT Strategy?

☐   Improve operational productivity and performance

☐   Reduction in customers served

☐   Price and inventory co-ordination

☐   Linked computer systems

☐   Create competitive advantage

☐   Enable structural change

☐   Bring congruency to corporate goals

---

21   **Relocating a department to another country within the region of the company's operations to take advantage of cost savings related to lower labour or infrastructure costs is known as which of the following?**

Select the most relevant option.

☐   Outsourcing

☐   Offshoring

☐   Near-shoring

☐   Franchising

22　There are many different bases for segmentation.

Which THREE of the following might be valid for segmentation of industrial and commercial customers?

☐　Level of income

☐　Demographic

☐　Location

☐　Socio-economic

☐　Ordering characteristics

☐　Expectations

23　**From a corporate governance perspective, which of the following is the key difference between large companies quoted on the stock exchange compared with a smaller, owner-managed company?**

Select the most relevant option.

☐　Domination by a single individual

☐　Poor cash flow management

☐　Ineffective management reporting

☐　Emphasis on short-term profitability

☐　Knowledge gap

24　**Which of the following is the key feature of a sales orientation that differentiates the organisation from one with a marketing orientation?**

Select the most relevant option.

☐　Focus on satisfying customer needs and wants

☐　Assumption that the customer can be persuaded to purchase given the right information

☐　Assumption that customers make buying decisions

☐　Collection and dissemination of customer information throughout the business

☐　Strategic and day-to-day decisions are made inter-departmentally

25　**A system that collects and integrates data from internal and external sources to create summarised information is known as:**

Select the most relevant option.

☐　Management Information System

☐　Executive Information System

☐　Decision Support System

☐　Knowledge Work System

☐　Office Automation System

☐　Expert System

26   **When planning the implementation of a new information system, the file conversion aspect involves which THREE of the following?**

☐   Users are involved to check data entry processes

☐   Master data maintenance documentation is created

☐   Data held in manual files will be keyed into the new system

☐   Data held in the existing computer files need to be converted to a format compatible with the new system

☐   Missing data is researched and made available for entry into the new system

27   **The daily work that takes place on production or assembly lines can be considered to be operating which of the following systems?**

Select the most relevant option.

☐   Feedback control system

☐   Open system

☐   Closed system

☐   Semi-closed system

28   **Which of the following is a feature of a process position layout from an employee's perspective?**

Select the most relevant option.

☐   There is a lot of movement of materials and resources

☐   Products flow through the factory using a variety of routes

☐   Small flexible machines are used to create specific individual products

☐   Resources are placed to maximise product flow

29   **To be successful, a corporate website should provide multiple features and functions. Which of the following would be an unpopular feature?**

Select the most relevant option.

☐   Attract visitors

☐   Enable participation

☐   Encourage return visits

☐   Allow for two-way information sharing

☐   Data capture for marketing campaigns

☐   Integrate with back office systems

☐   Security

30 **Duplication of tasks is least likely to occur in which of the following organisational structures?**

Select the most relevant option.

☐ Transitional

☐ Project

☐ Matrix

☐ Functional

31 **If an employee who is opposing the introduction of a new system is invited to user-acceptance testing, this is an example of which of the following:**

Select the most relevant option.

☐ Education

☐ Participation

☐ Negotiation

☐ Implicit coercion

32 Search engine optimisation is becoming increasingly important to marketers to ensure that the organisation's website appears high up in the search rankings.

Which of the following aspects of this may be perceived as a disadvantage to the organisation?

Select the most relevant option.

☐ Increased web traffic

☐ Trackable and quantifiable results

☐ Results based on years of search engine analytics

☐ Targeting of users who are actively looking for your products and services online

☐ Website becomes more navigable for users

☐ Increased exposure for your website and brand

33 **A flat organisation is characterised by which ONE of the following features:**

☐ Narrow control spans

☐ A large number of steps on the promotional ladders

☐ More opportunity for delegation

☐ Slow decision making and responses

☐ Rigid supervision can be imposed

34 **Which of the following would be regarded as an example of 'soft' human resource management in an organisation?**

Select the most relevant option.

☐ Little empowerment or delegation

☐ There is a competitive performance related pay structure

☐ Pay is sufficient to recruit and retain enough staff

☐ Appraisal systems focused on making judgements about staff

☐ Taller organisational structures

☐ Employees are a resource like plant and machinery

35 The definition of a quality circle has now expanded beyond a team of workers from within the organisation to also now include groups drawn from separate organisations which meets at regular intervals to discuss issues relating to the quality of the product or service produced.

Which TWO of the following are benefits of quality circles?

☐ Employee involvement improves morale

☐ Solutions are practical and effective

☐ Business practicalities may not be considered

☐ The scope of influence can be very wide

36 There are a number of ways of validating and evaluating a training scheme.

Which of the following would not be used to assess the effectiveness of a staff training event?

Select the most relevant option.

☐ Courses assessment sheets asking trainees if they thought the programme was useful

☐ Issue a test at the start of a training event

☐ Issue a test at the end of the training event

☐ Issue a test sometime after the training event

☐ Assess changes in job behaviour following training

37 **Which of the following processes is most commonly used in the manufacture of chemicals by the well-known global brands?**

Select the most relevant option.

☐ Jobbing

☐ Batch

☐ Mass

☐ Continuous

38 **What is the implication of Kolb's learning cycle theory?**

Select the most relevant option.

☐ For learning to be effective it must be examined

☐ For learning to be effective it must be reinforced by experience

☐ For learning to be effective it must be conducted off-site by external trainers

☐ For learning to be effective it must be conducted on-site by more experienced employees

39 **Which TWO of the following features are normally associated with the advantages of a decentralised organisational structure?**

☐ Better security over data and files

☐ Localised power to act

☐ Closeness to the customer

☐ A dominating head office

☐ Head office is in a better position to know what is going on

☐ Economies of scale realised in purchasing resources for the business

40 Mintzberg believes that all organisations can be analysed into five components, according to how they relate to the work of the organisation and how they prefer to co-ordinate.

What is the function of the technostructure?

Select the most relevant option.

☐ People directly involved in the process of obtaining inputs, and converting them into outputs

☐ Ancillary services such as IT

☐ Converts the desires of the strategic apex into the work done by the operating core

☐ Analysers determine the best way of doing a job

☐ Ensures the organisation follows its mission

41 Knowledge Work Systems (KWS) help knowledge workers create new knowledge and expertise.

Which of the following is NOT an example of a KWS?

Select the most relevant option.

☐ Digital filing systems

☐ Computer Aided Design (CAD)

☐ Computer Aided Manufacturing (CAM)

☐ Specialised financial software that analyses trading situations

42 **At the strategic level, payment systems have which THREE goals?**

☐ Create a pay range attached to particular levels of job grade

☐ Encourage performance and progression through development

☐ Aid staff recruitment

☐ Aid staff retention

☐ Ensure salary costs are controlled

☐ Reward employees for performance

43 Different organisations take different stances on social responsibility and this is reflected in how they manage such responsibilities.

Which of the following is NOT a corporate social responsibility stance identified by Johnson, Scholes & Whittington?

Select the most relevant option.

☐ Laissez-faire

☐ Enlightened self-interest

☐ Self-actualisation

☐ Multiple stakeholder obligations

☐ Shaper of society

44   Office Automation Systems (OAS) are computer systems designed to increase productivity of data and information workers.

Which of the following is an example of an OAS?

Select the most relevant option.

☐   Digital filing systems

☐   Computer Aided Design (CAD)

☐   Computer Aided Manufacturing (CAM)

☐   Specialised financial software that analyses trading situations

45   Enlightened self-interest is one of the four corporate social responsibility stances identified by Johnson, Scholes & Whittington.

Which of the following most closely describes this stance?

Select the most relevant option.

☐   Recognising that without appropriate relationships with groups such as suppliers, employers and customers, they would not be able to function

☐   Ensuring that society benefits from their actions is more important than financial and other stakeholder interests

☐   Organisations adopting this view believe that it is government's role to prescribe, through legislation and regulation, the constraints which are placed on businesses in their pursuit of economic efficiency

☐   The responsible exercise of corporate power may prevent a build-up of social and political pressure for legal regulation

46   The product life cycle considers five phases of a product life cycle.

Which FOUR of the following are not phases of the product life cycle?

☐   Maturity

☐   Decline

☐   Fall-out

☐   Growth

☐   Sales

☐   Market share

☐   Development

☐   Introduction

47   **Which of the following is associated with financial accounting?**

Select the most relevant option.

☐   Cash management

☐   Managing financial risks

☐   Raising finance

☐   Asset control

48   **A variety of techniques may be used in selection, and those chosen in a particular circumstance must be which FOUR of the following:**

☐   Accurately predict performance of employees

☐   Non-discriminating

☐   Generate consistent results

☐   Employment of unsuitable applicants

☐   Rejection of suitable applicants

☐   Costs of selection must be justified by the benefits of obtaining good quality staff

49   **From a retailer's point of view which of the following is the main reason for branding products or services?**

Select the most relevant option.

☐   Brand extension

☐   Maximises impact of advertising

☐   Justifies premium pricing

☐   Readier customer acceptance

☐   Aids product differentiation

☐   It eases the task of personal selling

50   The Ansoff matrix can be used to determine the possible strategies for products and markets.

Which FOUR of the following are represented by quadrants in the matrix?

☐   Market penetration

☐   Market decline

☐   Product fall-out

☐   Product growth

☐   Diversification

☐   Product development

☐   Market share

☐   Market development

☐   Introduction

51   **Which of the following is an advantage of a one-to-one recruitment and selection interview?**

Select the most relevant option.

☐   Can allow a rapport to build

☐   A general judgement can be based on a single attribute

☐   Involving more than one interviewer could result in differing opinions

☐   Interviewers can change the behaviour of the applicant through the wording of questions or non-verbal clues

☐   Abstract qualities are very difficult to assess

52 From the list below select TWO examples of a merit good:

☐ Free education

☐ Free healthcare

☐ Membership to a health club

☐ Drive safely campaigns

☐ Eat healthily campaigns

53 Which THREE of the following are potential advantages of self-appraisals?

☐ Subordinates tend to know their superior better than superiors know their subordinates

☐ People are often not the best judges of their own performance

☐ It saves the manager time

☐ Reduces the managerial role in appraisal

☐ Offers increased responsibility to the individual

54 Which FOUR of the following are examples of waste that the lean production improvement process aims to systematically eliminate?

☐ Early production

☐ Just-in-time processing

☐ Economies of scope

☐ Idle time

☐ Multiple handling

☐ Rework

55 Which organisational configuration was identified by Mintzberg as an effective way to manage large, complex organisations with control being exercised via performance measures such as profit?

Select the most relevant option.

☐ Matrix structure

☐ Centralised organisation

☐ Functional structure

☐ Divisionalised form

56 Write the appropriate word, chosen from the list below, in each space to complete the following statement:

A " _____ " supply chain is made up of the physical " _____ " linked together to

facilitate the " _____ " of goods and services to the final " _____ " .

a. Traditional
b. Entities
c. Supply
d. Demand
e. Consumer
f. Conservative

57   The work of Elton Mayo and Tom Lupton has shown that there are several constraints which prevent most people from seeking to maximise their earnings.

Which of the following is NOT a constraint to people maximising their earnings?

Select the most relevant option.

☐   Work groups tend to restrict output to a level that they feel is fair and safe.

☐   Workers conform to a group output norm

☐   Workers are unlikely to be in complete control of results

☐   Workers are capable of influencing the timings and control systems used by management

---

58   **Which of the following is NOT a feature of business to business marketing?**

Select the most relevant option.

☐   Organisational markets normally comprise more buyers

☐   Technically complex transactions

☐   Higher financial value than consumers

☐   Purchasing decision is made by consensus

---

59   **Which of the following is NOT a type of psychological contract?**

Select the most relevant option.

☐   Co-operative

☐   Coercive

☐   Calculative

☐   Co-optation

---

60   **The integrative phase of Reck and Long's model of the evolution of the purchasing function is characterised by which THREE features?**

☐   This phase is often characterised by a centralised purchasing department with organisation-wide buying policies and systems

☐   The importance of careful supplier selection is recognised

☐   Pro-active purchasing strategies are developed and followed

☐   A more professional approach to purchasing is taken

☐   Suppliers are viewed as partners and supplier management is viewed as relationship management

☐   Purchasing is now fully integrated in the major business activities of the organisation

Practice mock answers

Answers

1   The correct answer is: The opening or closure of workplaces competing for the same skills.

The closure of workplaces competing for the same skills would reduce demand for those skills in that region.

The opening of workplaces competing for the same skills would increase demand for those skills in that region.

The availability of government funding for training schemes may increase supply if the training is for those same skills, but it will not increase demand for those skills.

A change in factory shift patterns is likely to impact unskilled labour, but is unlikely to affect skilled labour.

The availability, or supply of skilled labour, will affect the wage rates but not the demand for skilled labour.

---

2   The correct answer is: Industry, type, size, structure.

Industry   The pharmaceutical industry would require more rigorous data capture, product costing, batch number tracking and reporting capabilities than an accounting system for the pottery industry where unit cost per product would be important but not necessarily tracking per batch of input through to delivered customer.

Type   A service business might need to record the time employees take on particular jobs. Accounting on a job or client basis might also be a feature of service businesses. A public sector organisation, such as a government department, may be more concerned with the monitoring of expenditure against performance targets than recording revenue. A manufacturing company will account both for unit sales and revenue, but needs to keep track of costs for decision-making purposes and so forth.

Size   A small business like a greengrocer will have a simple accounting system, where the main accounting record will probably be the till roll. A large retail business, such as a chain of supermarkets, will have elaborate accounting systems covering a large number of product ranges and sites.

Structure   In a business managed by area, accounts will be prepared on an area basis. In a functional organisation, the accounts staff are in a separate department.

Degree of decentralisation, manager performance and motivation, and the requirement to provide information to external parties will all impact the way in which the system is used, but are unlikely to determine the complexity and scope of the accounting system.

---

3   The correct answers are:

*   Writing an article for a trade journal; or
*   Posting 'blogs' online to draw attention to the organisation.

A common example is food magazines including 'advertising features' in the form of recipes which use a particular producer's products.

Targeting individual customers with promotional material is a form of direct marketing because there are no other parties between the seller and the customer.

Providing free e-books on social media sites is a form of viral marketing because it relies on the use of pre-existing social networks to spread brand awareness or other marketing objectives by attracting attention with a free product or service.

---

4   The correct answer is: Velocity.

Velocity refers to the speed at which 'real time' data is being streamed into the organisation. To make data meaningful it needs to be processed in a reasonable time frame.

Variation in demand and visibility are features of the four Vs of operation, used to analyse the differences between transformational processes.

Value added refers to organisational activities that add value to the customers and therefore reduce the threat of substitutes.

---

5   The correct answer is: Improved communication with customers and suppliers enables stakeholders to collaborate more readily.

The value of commercial software increases and more competition among suppliers are not advantages for the enterprise, although competition amongst suppliers may be an advantage for customers if this means reduced prices at similar or higher quality.

The networked enterprise does not necessarily have access to up to date processes as this will depend upon how up to date the other organisations are within the network.

---

6   The correct answer is: Expertise is pooled thanks to the division of work into specialist areas.

Horizontal coordination across the functions is often impeded by the vertical barriers to information and work flow created by functional structures. It is not easy in a functional structure.

Hierarchy overload can occur as it is caused by the vertical hierarchy becoming isolated, with decisions piling up as top managers lack effective means of coordination across specialist functions.

A good level of communication between different functions is hindered, with each function often having their own jargon.

Functional structures result in less innovation due to the focus on specialist tasks, not cross-functional working.

Focuses on internal processes and inputs, rather than the customer and outputs, which are what ultimately drive the business. Inward-looking businesses are less able to adapt to changing demands and this is therefore a disadvantage of a functional structure.

---

7   The correct answer is: The acid test ratio and the current ratio are liquidity ratios. They are used to determine a company's ability to pay off its short-term debt obligations. Generally, the higher the value of the ratio, the more likely it is that the company will be able to cover its short-term debts without difficulty.

Earnings per share, Price/earnings ratio and Dividend yield are all investor ratios, used to determine how well the company is performing to provide a return for its investors.

Stock turn is an asset turnover ratio, used to indicate how efficiently the firm utilises its assets.

Profit per employee and return on sales are both operating performance ratios used to assess management performance for efficient operations.

---

8   The correct answer is: Product, Promotion, Price, Production.

Product, Promotion and Price are three of the 4Ps of the marketing mix.

Marketing has three dimensions:

It is a culture. The marketing concept is to focus on consumer needs.

It involves strategy. A company must select the markets it intends to sell to and the products or services it will sell. These selections are strategic decisions.

It involves tactics. Marketing tactics can be considered as the 7Ps of the marketing mix.

9   The correct answer is: It is publically available. Whilst the code of ethics is generally aimed at and used by the company employees, to be effective it needs to be available to anybody with an interest in the company's activities and the way it does business. This will help ensure that the company and its employees are operating in line with the values and principles set out in the code of ethics across all business and community activities.

A number of factors, including the company values, may be considered when determining whether something is ethically right or wrong. This does not mean that the company values need to be part of the written code of ethics.

Compliance should be rewarded, not non-compliance.

Ethical principles are not necessarily enforced by law, although the law incorporates moral judgements.

10   The correct answer is: Printing on recycled paper is both ethical and legal.

Working with competitors to ensure the market remains profitable would suggest price fixing or operating as part of a cartel. This is unethical and illegal.

Targeting young adults in an 'alcopops' advertising campaign is unethical, but legal.

Highlighting onerous contract clauses included in the small print is a legal requirement, but it is unethical to include onerous clauses in contracts regardless of whether or not they are highlighted.

Passing off cheap imitation goods as designer brands is unethical and illegal.

11   The correct answer is: The suppliers and resources are also available to rival operations. This is a disadvantage of the virtual organisation as the company cannot gain a competitive advantage by securing supply or resources solely for their use and therefore their competitors also have access to them.

Improved flexibility and speed of operation, low investment in assets and hence less risk involves and injection of market forces into all the linkages in the value chain are all advantages of virtual operations.

12   The correct answer is: Setting up an effective shared service level agreement is one of the biggest challenges as the use of the shared service centres is mandatory, with the scope of resources of the business unit being reduced yet they are still accountable for the same business performance.

Shared service centres aim to achieve significant cost reductions while improving service levels through the use of standardised technology and processes and service level agreements.

13   The correct answer is:

The company operates a share save scheme where employees become shareholders in the company – this means that the existing shareholders and the employees (new/future shareholders) have a common interest in the success and growth of the business.

Suppliers work in collaboration with the business on new product design to meet customer demands for product improvement – this meets the needs of the customer, ensures future sales for the supplier (and potentially increased sales if the new product improves sales growth) and the company makes more sale (and possibly more profitable sales) which provides for higher dividends for shareholders.

Directors introduce a corporate social responsibility charter which increases its involvement in the local community – this benefits the local community, may benefit employees wanting to have more involvement in community events and could be used in marketing campaigns to increase the customer base and therefore improve profitability which benefits shareholders.

14   The correct answer is: It provides the ability to more quickly upgrade products with advanced technology and quality features – this is a benefit of the product orientation. Although more responsive to customer needs, companies with a marketing orientation do not prioritise product improvement and this can be a deterrent to cutting-edge buyers who want to get in on the latest product advances.

It promotes and delivers desired products and services. The marketing concept begins by identifying the customer need, and then developing products or services to meet that need.

It provides practical information to assist customers in making a purchase, such as addresses, telephone numbers, website addresses, product release dates and store hours.

It helps set and manage consumer expectations, by businesses using marketing to make consumers aware of major changes that affect product offerings.

It provides a place for behavioural research. The government can make use of consumer behaviour analysis when crafting awareness campaigns for major public and social issues.

15   The correct answer is: Observe the highest standards of conduct and integrity, uphold the good standing and reputation of the profession and refrain from any conduct which might discredit the profession.

Ensure consistency is upheld in operating practices – just because a task has always been performed in a certain way does not mean that it is an ethical practice and this should be challenged when encountered by a CIMA member.

Base decision making on the primary stakeholder affected by the decision – pressure from supervisors, friends and relatives or key stakeholders can be a difficult conflict to be managed by a CIMA member and should be referred up the organisation's hierarchy or CIMA can be consulted for the ethical course of action.

16   The correct answer is: Feedback.

Feedforward control systems use forecast, rather than historic, results to take action during the financial period.

Open loop control systems do not observe the output of the process it is controlling and focuses only on the current state and its model of the system.

Activity based control systems are based on the activity-based costing methodology.

17   The correct answer is: Dominance by a single senior executive, irregular board meetings, lack of employee supervision and director bonus schemes based on company performance such as profitability (creating an emphasis on short-term profitability) have all been instrumental in past high profile corporate scandals and collapses.

An audit committee comprised entirely of non-executive directors may be regarded as an important safeguard in ensuring that the organisation has effective controls in place and that they are upheld.

Segregation of key roles ensures that one individual does not have control over the whole end-to-end process and therefore there is the ability for another individual to question the validity and level of corporate exposure created by the actions being undertaken.

18   The correct answer is: Financial ratio analysis, effective taxation administration and reporting on variances between the expected and actual financial results.

Financial ratio analysis is part of the financial accounting function.

Effective taxation administration is part of the treasury function.

Reporting on variances between the expected and actual financial results is part of the management accounting function.

19   The correct answer is: Differing management styles and operational models used are likely to cause arguments over how the business should operate.

Marketing and other advice and support is provided – this is for franchise operations.

Acting in a certain geographical location as a distribution channel – this is an agent arrangement.

20   The correct answer is: Improve operational productivity and performance, create competitive advantage, enable structural change and bring congruency to corporate goals.

Reduction in customers served, price and inventory co-ordination and linked computer systems are all benefits of optimising supply chain management.

21   The correct answer is: Near-shoring is a form of offshoring but the department is relocated to a country within the region of the business.

Outsourcing involves an organisation sub-contracting its business activities to external providers who may be in the same country as the organisation, or based overseas.

Offshoring is the relocation of some part of an organisation's activities to another country.

Franchising is the setting up of a licensing agreement for other companies to sell the franchisor's products or provide their services.

22   The correct answer is: Location, ordering characteristics and expectations.

Level of income, demographic and socio-economic could all be suitable bases to segment consumer markets based on individuals.

23   The correct answer is: The 'knowledge gap' or 'agency problem' is caused by the shareholders not having access to the day-to-day company management information and therefore having to rely on the directors to act in their interest.

Domination by a single individual is a problem that can arise in large organisations where a senior executive dominates the board, with the other board members merely acting as a rubber stamp.

Emphasis on short-term results can lead to the concealment of problems or errors, or manipulation of accounts to achieve desired results in large organisations. In small owner-managed organisations it may risk the longevity of the enterprise.

Poor cash flow management and ineffective management reporting can occur in organisations of any size and management structure.

24   The correct answer is:

Assumption that the customer can be persuaded to purchase given the right information – a sales orientation looks inward at the business and its need to sell products or services. The assumption is that customers are reluctant to purchase but that a good sales force can sell just about anything to anybody.

25   The correct answer is: An executive information system (EIS) pools data from internal and external sources and makes information available to senior managers in an easy-to-use form. EIS help senior managers make strategic, unstructured decisions.

Management information systems (MIS) convert data from mainly internal sources into information (eg summary reports, exception reports). This information enables managers to make timely and effective decisions for planning, directing and controlling the activities for which they are responsible.

Decision support systems (DSS) combine data and analytical models or data analysis tools to support semi-structured and unstructured decision making.

Knowledge work systems (KWS) are information systems that facilitate the creation and integration of new knowledge into an organisation.

Office automation systems (OAS) are computer systems designed to increase the productivity of data and information workers.

Expert systems are a form of DSS that allow users to benefit from expert knowledge and information. Such systems consist of a database holding specialised data and rules about what to do in, or how to interpret, a given set of circumstances.

---

26   The correct answer is: Data held in manual files will be keyed into the new system, data held in the existing computer files need to be converted to a format compatible with the new system and missing data is researched and made available for entry into the new system.

Users are involved to check data entry processes – this is a type of realistic testing, not file conversion.

Master data maintenance documentation is created – this is part of the training and documentation aspect of the systems implementation project.

---

27   The correct answer is: A closed system is a system which is isolated from its environment and independent of it. The workers on an assembly line are generally only responsible for completing their tasks on the line and are insulated from outside factors such as meetings between upper-level executives or competing production lines.

Feedback control system describes the situation where part of system output is returned (fed-back) as an input.

An open system is a system connected to and interacting with its environment. It takes in influences (or 'energy') from its environment and also influences this environment by its behaviour (it exports energy).

A semi-closed system interfaces with the environment and reacts in a predictable, controlled way. This differs from an open system as open systems interact with the environment in both a controlled and uncontrolled way.

---

28   The correct answer is: Products flow through the factory using a variety of routes.

There is a lot of movement of materials and resources – this is a feature of a fixed layout.

Small flexible machines are used to create specific individual products – this is a feature of a cell layout.

Resources are placed to maximise product flow – this is a feature of a product layout.

---

29   The correct answer is: Data capture for marketing campaigns – the organisation's reputation will be damaged if confidential customer information is lost or sold onto third parties without prior consent.

---

30   The correct answer is: Functional – expertise is pooled into specialist areas which avoids duplication and enables economies of scale.

The other three structures all have potential for duplication to be introduced.

---

31   The correct answer is: Participation – where those affected by the change have the power to resist it, this method reduces the resistance by taking their views into account.

Education – this method is effective where the cause of the resistance is lack of information about the change.

Negotiation – compensating those who lose out (for example redundancy packages).

Implicit coercion – this involves the use or threat of force to push through the change.

---

32   The correct answer is: Results based on years of search engine analytics – but the organisation has no control of how much traffic is generated or what types of traffic is received.

---

33   The correct answer is: More opportunity for delegation.

All the other points are features of a tall organisation.

34   The correct answer is: There is a competitive performance related pay structure – Soft HRM views employees as the organisation's most important asset and as a source of competitive advantage. HR effort should be high with staff being empowered and competitive rates of pay offered (performance should be rewarded).

Hard HRM views employees as a resource just like tools and equipment. Hard HRM suggests that empowerment of employees should not be encouraged and HR effort should be limited to recruiting and retaining staff.

35   The correct answer is: Employee involvement improves morale as the employees feel empowered and their contribution is valued. Solutions are practical and likely to be effective as workers know the processes involved.

Disadvantages:

Business practicalities may not be considered as the workers are generally from low level roles and so they may not understand the wider implications or cost implications of their solutions.

The scope of influence can become very wide and it can be difficult to control employee power.

36   The correct answer is: Issue a test at the start of a training event – this is only useful when used in conjunction with testing immediately or sometime after the training event.

37   The correct answer is: Continuous – the manufacture of products requiring sequential performance of different processes on a series of multiple machines receiving the material for manufacture through a closed channel.

38   The correct answer is: For learning to be effective it must be reinforced by experience.

39   The correct answer is: Localised power to act and closeness to the customer ensure a faster response to customer or local market requirements and this can be a source of competitive advantage.

The other points are advantages of a centralised organisational structure.

40   The correct answer is: Analysers determine the best way of doing a job.

People directly involved in the process of obtaining inputs, and converting them into outputs – Operating core.

Ancillary services such as IT – Support staff.

Converts the desires of the strategic apex into the work done by the operating core – Middle Line.

Ensures the organisation follows its mission – Strategic Apex.

41   The correct answer is: Digital filing systems are an example of an Office Automation System (OAS).

42   The correct answer is: Aid staff recruitment, aid staff retention and reward employees for performance.

A pay range is a type of pay structure, not a goal of payment systems.

Encourage performance and progression through development and ensuring salary costs are controlled are both goals of a payment system at the managerial level.

43   The correct answer is: Self-actualisation is the fulfilment of personal potential that Maslow discussed as never being satisfied in his theory on the hierarchy of needs.

44   The correct answer is: Digital filing systems.

The other three points are examples of Knowledge Work Systems.

45 The correct answer is: The responsible exercise of corporate power may prevent a build-up of social and political pressure for legal regulation.

Recognising that without appropriate relationships with groups such as suppliers, employers and customers, they would not be able to function. This is the multiple stakeholder stance.

Ensuring that society benefits from their actions is more important than financial and other stakeholder interests. This is the shaper of society stance.

Organisations adopting this view believe that it is government's role to prescribe, through legislation and regulation, the constraints which are placed on businesses in their pursuit of economic efficiency. This is the laissez-faire stance.

46 The correct answer is: Fall-out, Sales, Market share and Development.

47 The correct answer is: Asset control.

The other points are associated with treasury management.

48 The correct answer is:

Reliable – generate consistent results.

Valid – accurately predict performance of employees.

Fair – non-discriminating.

Cost-effective – the benefits of obtaining good quality staff must justify the costs of selecting them.

Employment of unsuitable applicants and rejection of suitable applicants would be the results of an ineffective selection process.

49 The correct answer is: It eases the task of personal selling by enhancing product recognition.

The other points are important from a manufacture's point of view.

50 The correct answer is: Market penetration, Market development, Product development and Diversification.

Market penetration involves increasing sales of the existing products in existing markets.

Market development entails expansion into new markets using existing products.

Product development involves the redesign or repositioning of existing products or the introduction of completely new ones in order to appeal to existing markets.

Diversification involves producing new products for new markets. It is much more risky than the other three because the organisation is moving into areas in which it has little or no experience.

51 The correct answer is: Can allow a rapport to build.

52 The correct answer is: Free education and free healthcare.

Merit goods are goods or services provided free for the benefit of society by the government.

Demerit goods are those considered by the government to be unhealthy or damaging to society. A social marketing campaign would encourage people to drive safely or eat healthily.

53 The correct answer is: It saves the manager time, reduces the managerial role in appraisal and offers increased responsibility to the individual.

Subordinates tend to know their superior better than superiors know their subordinates – this is an advantage of an upward appraisal.

People are often not the best judges of their own performance – this is a disadvantage of self-appraisals.

54   The correct answer is: Early production, idle time, multiple handling and rework.

Just-in-time processing, economies of scope and active involvement of workers are all characteristics of lean production.

55   The correct answer is: Divisionalised form.

56   The correct answer is:

A <u>traditional</u> supply chain is made up of the physical <u>entities</u> linked together to facilitate the <u>supply</u> of goods and services to the final <u>consumer</u>.

57   The correct answer is: Workers are unlikely to be in complete control of results – this is a potential difficulty of incentive schemes.

58   The correct answer is: Organisational markets normally comprise more buyers – usually there are fewer buyers, with a few buyers responsible for the majority of sales.

Size of orders, quality and service level agreements can make B2B transactions complex technically.

Businesses have greater purchasing power than consumers and can afford.

The purchase decision is usually made by consensus in an organisational setting, rather than being the responsibility of one person.

59   The correct answer is: Co-optation – this is a method of dealing with user resistance. This method involves the presentation of partial or misleading information to those resisting change or 'buying-off' the main individuals who are at the heart of the resistance.

Coercive contract – this is a contract in which the individual considers that they are being forced to contribute their efforts and energies involuntarily, and that the rewards they receive in return are inadequate compensation.

Calculative contract – this is a contract, accepted voluntarily by the individual, in which they expect to do their job in exchange for a readily identifiable set of rewards. With such psychological contracts, motivation can only be increased if the rewards to the individual are improved.

Co-operative contract – this is a contract in which the individual identifies themselves with the organisation and its goals, so that they actively seek to contribute further to the achievement of those goals. Motivation comes out of success at work, a sense of achievement, and self-fulfilment.

60   The correct answer is: Pro-active purchasing strategies are developed and followed, suppliers are viewed as partners and supplier management is viewed as relationship management and purchasing is now fully integrated in the major business activities of the organisation.

A more professional approach to purchasing is taken is a characteristic of the independent phase.

This phase is often characterised by a centralised purchasing department with organisation-wide buying policies and systems and the importance of careful supplier selection is recognised are characteristics of the supportive phase.

Mathematical tables

PRESENT VALUE TABLE

Present value of 1.00 unit of currency, that is $(1+r)^{-n}$ where r = interest rate; n = number of periods until payment or receipt.

Periods	Interest rates (r)									
(n)	1%	2%	3%	4%	5%	6%	7%	8%	9%	10%
1	0.990	0.980	0.971	0.962	0.952	0.943	0.935	0.926	0.917	0.909
2	0.980	0.961	0.943	0.925	0.907	0.890	0.873	0.857	0.842	0.826
3	0.971	0.942	0.915	0.889	0.864	0.840	0.816	0.794	0.772	0.751
4	0.961	0.924	0.888	0.855	0.823	0.792	0.763	0.735	0.708	0.683
5	0.951	0.906	0.863	0.822	0.784	0.747	0.713	0.681	0.650	0.621
6	0.942	0.888	0.837	0.790	0.746	0.705	0.666	0.630	0.596	0.564
7	0.933	0.871	0.813	0.760	0.711	0.665	0.623	0.583	0.547	0.513
8	0.923	0.853	0.789	0.731	0.677	0.627	0.582	0.540	0.502	0.467
9	0.914	0.837	0.766	0.703	0.645	0.592	0.544	0.500	0.460	0.424
10	0.905	0.820	0.744	0.676	0.614	0.558	0.508	0.463	0.422	0.386
11	0.896	0.804	0.722	0.650	0.585	0.527	0.475	0.429	0.388	0.350
12	0.887	0.788	0.701	0.625	0.557	0.497	0.444	0.397	0.356	0.319
13	0.879	0.773	0.681	0.601	0.530	0.469	0.415	0.368	0.326	0.290
14	0.870	0.758	0.661	0.577	0.505	0.442	0.388	0.340	0.299	0.263
15	0.861	0.743	0.642	0.555	0.481	0.417	0.362	0.315	0.275	0.239
16	0.853	0.728	0.623	0.534	0.458	0.394	0.339	0.292	0.252	0.218
17	0.844	0.714	0.605	0.513	0.436	0.371	0.317	0.270	0.231	0.198
18	0.836	0.700	0.587	0.494	0.416	0.350	0.296	0.250	0.212	0.180
19	0.828	0.686	0.570	0.475	0.396	0.331	0.277	0.232	0.194	0.164
20	0.820	0.673	0.554	0.456	0.377	0.312	0.258	0.215	0.178	0.149

Periods	Interest rates (r)									
(n)	11%	12%	13%	14%	15%	16%	17%	18%	19%	20%
1	0.901	0.893	0.885	0.877	0.870	0.862	0.855	0.847	0.840	0.833
2	0.812	0.797	0.783	0.769	0.756	0.743	0.731	0.718	0.706	0.694
3	0.731	0.712	0.693	0.675	0.658	0.641	0.624	0.609	0.593	0.579
4	0.659	0.636	0.613	0.592	0.572	0.552	0.534	0.516	0.499	0.482
5	0.593	0.567	0.543	0.519	0.497	0.476	0.456	0.437	0.419	0.402
6	0.535	0.507	0.480	0.456	0.432	0.410	0.390	0.370	0.352	0.335
7	0.482	0.452	0.425	0.400	0.376	0.354	0.333	0.314	0.296	0.279
8	0.434	0.404	0.376	0.351	0.327	0.305	0.285	0.266	0.249	0.233
9	0.391	0.361	0.333	0.308	0.284	0.263	0.243	0.225	0.209	0.194
10	0.352	0.322	0.295	0.270	0.247	0.227	0.208	0.191	0.176	0.162
11	0.317	0.287	0.261	0.237	0.215	0.195	0.178	0.162	0.148	0.135
12	0.286	0.257	0.231	0.208	0.187	0.168	0.152	0.137	0.124	0.112
13	0.258	0.229	0.204	0.182	0.163	0.145	0.130	0.116	0.104	0.093
14	0.232	0.205	0.181	0.160	0.141	0.125	0.111	0.099	0.088	0.078
15	0.209	0.183	0.160	0.140	0.123	0.108	0.095	0.084	0.079	0.065
16	0.188	0.163	0.141	0.123	0.107	0.093	0.081	0.071	0.062	0.054
17	0.170	0.146	0.125	0.108	0.093	0.080	0.069	0.060	0.052	0.045
18	0.153	0.130	0.111	0.095	0.081	0.069	0.059	0.051	0.044	0.038
19	0.138	0.116	0.098	0.083	0.070	0.060	0.051	0.043	0.037	0.031
20	0.124	0.104	0.087	0.073	0.061	0.051	0.043	0.037	0.031	0.026

Cumulative present value of 1.00 unit of currency per annum, Receivable or Payable at the end of each year for n years $\frac{1-(1+r)^{-n}}{r}$

Periods (n)	Interest rates (r)									
	1%	2%	3%	4%	5%	6%	7%	8%	9%	10%
1	0.990	0.980	0.971	0.962	0.952	0.943	0.935	0.926	0.917	0.909
2	1.970	1.942	1.913	1.886	1.859	1.833	1.808	1.783	1.759	1.736
3	2.941	2.884	2.829	2.775	2.723	2.673	2.624	2.577	2.531	2.487
4	3.902	3.808	3.717	3.630	3.546	3.465	3.387	3.312	3.240	3.170
5	4.853	4.713	4.580	4.452	4.329	4.212	4.100	3.993	3.890	3.791
6	5.795	5.601	5.417	5.242	5.076	4.917	4.767	4.623	4.486	4.355
7	6.728	6.472	6.230	6.002	5.786	5.582	5.389	5.206	5.033	4.868
8	7.652	7.325	7.020	6.733	6.463	6.210	5.971	5.747	5.535	5.335
9	8.566	8.162	7.786	7.435	7.108	6.802	6.515	6.247	5.995	5.759
10	9.471	8.983	8.530	8.111	7.722	7.360	7.024	6.710	6.418	6.145
11	10.368	9.787	9.253	8.760	8.306	7.887	7.499	7.139	6.805	6.495
12	11.255	10.575	9.954	9.385	8.863	8.384	7.943	7.536	7.161	6.814
13	12.134	11.348	10.635	9.986	9.394	8.853	8.358	7.904	7.487	7.103
14	13.004	12.106	11.296	10.563	9.899	9.295	8.745	8.244	7.786	7.367
15	13.865	12.849	11.938	11.118	10.380	9.712	9.108	8.559	8.061	7.606
16	14.718	13.578	12.561	11.652	10.838	10.106	9.447	8.851	8.313	7.824
17	15.562	14.292	13.166	12.166	11.274	10.477	9.763	9.122	8.544	8.022
18	16.398	14.992	13.754	12.659	11.690	10.828	10.059	9.372	8.756	8.201
19	17.226	15.679	14.324	13.134	12.085	11.158	10.336	9.604	8.950	8.365
20	18.046	16.351	14.878	13.590	12.462	11.470	10.594	9.818	9.129	8.514

Periods (n)	Interest rates (r)									
	11%	12%	13%	14%	15%	16%	17%	18%	19%	20%
1	0.901	0.893	0.885	0.877	0.870	0.862	0.855	0.847	0.840	0.833
2	1.713	1.690	1.668	1.647	1.626	1.605	1.585	1.566	1.547	1.528
3	2.444	2.402	2.361	2.322	2.283	2.246	2.210	2.174	2.140	2.106
4	3.102	3.037	2.974	2.914	2.855	2.798	2.743	2.690	2.639	2.589
5	3.696	3.605	3.517	3.433	3.352	3.274	3.199	3.127	3.058	2.991
6	4.231	4.111	3.998	3.889	3.784	3.685	3.589	3.498	3.410	3.326
7	4.712	4.564	4.423	4.288	4.160	4.039	3.922	3.812	3.706	3.605
8	5.146	4.968	4.799	4.639	4.487	4.344	4.207	4.078	3.954	3.837
9	5.537	5.328	5.132	4.946	4.772	4.607	4.451	4.303	4.163	4.031
10	5.889	5.650	5.426	5.216	5.019	4.833	4.659	4.494	4.339	4.192
11	6.207	5.938	5.687	5.453	5.234	5.029	4.836	4.656	4.486	4.327
12	6.492	6.194	5.918	5.660	5.421	5.197	4.988	4.793	4.611	4.439
13	6.750	6.424	6.122	5.842	5.583	5.342	5.118	4.910	4.715	4.533
14	6.982	6.628	6.302	6.002	5.724	5.468	5.229	5.008	4.802	4.611
15	7.191	6.811	6.462	6.142	5.847	5.575	5.324	5.092	4.876	4.675
16	7.379	6.974	6.604	6.265	5.954	5.668	5.405	5.162	4.938	4.730
17	7.549	7.120	6.729	6.373	6.047	5.749	5.475	5.222	4.990	4.775
18	7.702	7.250	6.840	6.467	6.128	5.818	5.534	5.273	5.033	4.812
19	7.839	7.366	6.938	6.550	6.198	5.877	5.584	5.316	5.070	4.843
20	7.963	7.469	7.025	6.623	6.259	5.929	5.628	5.353	5.101	4.870